BUTLER

Salena Zito

BUTLER

The Untold Story of the
Near Assassination of Donald Trump
and the Fight for America's Heartland

CENTER
STREET

Nashville – New York

Center Street
Hachette Book Group
1290 Avenue of the Americas, New York, NY 10104
centerstreet.com
@CenterStreet

First Edition: July 2025

Center Street is a division of Hachette Book Group, Inc. The Center Street name and logo are registered trademarks of Hachette Book Group, Inc.

The publisher is not responsible for websites (or their content) that are not owned by the publisher.

Center Street books may be purchased in bulk for business, educational, or promotional use.

For information, please contact your local bookseller or the Hachette Book Group Special Markets Department at special.markets@hbgusa.com.

All photos unless otherwise indicated are courtesy of the author's personal collection.

Library of Congress Cataloging-in-Publication Data has been applied for.

ISBN: 9781546009146 (hardcover), 9781546009160 (ebook), 9781668649909 (audio)

Printed in the United States of America

LSC

Printing 1, 2025

For my family: Mom and Dad, for leading by example;
Shannon and Glenn, for being a shining example of what it
means to raise good kids and for your ridiculous senses of humor;
Michael, for being a good husband to my daughter and
father to my grandchildren; and finally my grandchildren,
Eleanora, Milo, Louisa, and Rocco, who are my joys,
my loves, my everything.

Contents

Introduction

_____

They Shoot Presidents in Butler

George Washington was less than pleased.

It was December 26, 1753, well past dusk and the temperature had dropped dramatically as darkness fell. Thanks to the drop in temperature, the mix of sleet and snow would make travel perilous in the deeply forested wilderness of what is now present-day Butler County.

But Washington and his guide Christopher Gist were left with little choice; they had to move, and move quickly.

They needed to make their way to the forks of the Ohio River. Days later, Washington, then a young major in the Virginia militia, would write in his journal that fear coursed through his veins and spurred the urgency of their flight after he was nearly killed by an assassin's bullet that whizzed past his ear just hours earlier.

Both he and Gist knew his assassin would be back to finish the job.

At twenty-one years old, Washington was on his first diplomatic mission, with direct orders from the Crown tucked in his saddlebag to basically tell the French to get off King George II's land or face war with England.

In 1753, the British and French Empires were in the early stages of clashing over their colonial possessions. Britain's North American colonies were mostly packed along the Atlantic coastline and then moved westward toward the Allegheny Mountains.

France's colonial holdings were in the center spine of the country that began in New Orleans and ran up along the Mississippi River into the Great Lakes region toward the St. Lawrence River.

Both empires claimed control of the vast expanse of what was then known as the Ohio Country, which began in present-day western Pennsylvania and West Virginia and spread due west across the states of Ohio and Indiana.

Washington was at the center of that clash of royal aspirations, which were largely spurred by greed in the form of an immense royal grant to the Ohio Company, whose largest investor was Robert Dinwiddie, Virginia's royal (lieutenant) governor and the man who sent Washington on the mission.

The young Virginian's destination was Fort Le Boeuf, just fifteen miles south of Lake Erie. In Washington's possession was a note from London, signed by King George II, that read: "If the French were found to be building forts on English soil, they should be peacefully asked to depart. If they failed to comply, however, we do hereby strictly charge and command you to drive them off by force of arms."[1]

The trip from Virginia had been a daunting 250 miles of untouched wilderness. It involved scaling high ice-crusted ridges, slogging through thick brush, swamps, and dense forests with mounds of heavy snow, and navigating icy waterways. The journey was as difficult as one could imagine, not just because of the terrain but also because of a weather system that had pummeled Washington and Gist the entire way.

Washington arrived at Fort Le Boeuf on December 11. The fort system was rudimentary at best, made of scrap bark and planks and consisting of four buildings. The young soldier and French commander Capt. Jacques Legardeur de Saint-Pierre had a cordial, diplomatic conversation despite Washington's delivery of the Crown's demand that the French vacate the Ohio Valley immediately.

Saint-Pierre made clear that he was not intimidated by the British and retained every right to arrest their traders who were poaching on French territory. "As to the summons you sent me to retire, I do not think myself obliged to obey it."[2]

Four days later, Saint-Pierre handed Washington a sealed message for Dinwiddie. It was then that Washington discovered that, although Saint-Pierre had filled Washington's canoe with a generous amount of supplies for the journey home, the French commander had also bribed Washington's Indian guides with food and drink to stay behind.

Washington was furious. He had not only been deceived by Saint-Pierre; he had also observed enough during his four-day wait for the commander to respond to Dinwiddie to know that France was building a large-scale fort system throughout the disputed territory. He also observed that they were building a formidable military operation, which was prepared to defend the land the French would take over.

Washington and Gist set off, anxious to deliver the news to Dinwiddie. However, their horses were so debilitated by the journey to Fort Le Boeuf that the men had to abandon them and continue on foot.

On the journey toward the outpost known as Murdering Town (in present-day Butler), they were heavily burdened by their backpacks. Along the way, they encountered several French Indians who quickly—probably too quickly, in hindsight—offered to help get them to the forks of the Ohio River. The battering snow and sleet, freezing cold, and rough terrain had worn Washington down, and when one of the Indian guides offered to carry his backpack, he took him up on it.

Gist, a skilled surveyor and frontier guide, immediately sensed something was off about the situation. He wasn't wrong. As soon as the group came to a clearing, one of the Indians sprinted ahead of them into a meadow and then turned to face the two men before firing point-blank at Washington from fifteen paces.

The exact amount by which the French-aligned Indian missed Washington is unclear. Washington's diary entry is vague, but the intent was obvious. The Indian guide wanted the young Virginian dead.[3]

If muskets had contained rifling—grooves inside the barrel to make a bullet travel more accurately—270 years ago, everything in the world would have changed at that moment.

There would have been no skirmish several months later in present-day Fayette County, Pennsylvania, between Washington's regiment and French soldiers—a skirmish that led to the first shots fired in what would quickly escalate into the French and Indian War. It was a war that ultimately led to the Revolutionary War, when the British Crown tried to tax the colonists to pay for debt incurred during the first true world war.

There would have been no General Washington, no President Washington, and we might not have the country we call America today if that bullet had been only an inch closer.

BUTLER

Chapter 1

One Inch Away

BUTLER, *Pennsylvania*

Pop.

  Pop.

  Pop.

  Pop.

I felt the velocity in the same split second that I heard the four gunshots. My eyes were fixated on former president Donald Trump, who stood a mere few feet away from me on an outdoor stage in front of the podium. It was July 13, 2024. I was in the buffer zone with my daughter, Shannon Venditti, and my son-in-law Michael.

Shannon looked over at me and asked, "Why are there fireworks?" I knew they weren't fireworks and, subconsciously, she did too. We are gun owners. Shannon didn't want to think this could be happening; a mother of four, she didn't want to believe we were in the line of fire. I heard her yell to Michael, "Did you trip on the speaker wires and cause them to spark?"

My gaze never left the president. Everything happened simultaneously, seemed to happen in split-second layers. I saw him flinch. He grabbed his ear. I saw the blood streak on his face as the bullets cut across the stage, and he ducked down below the podium.

"Get down, get down, get down!" a male voice shouted from behind me, directed at the president.

My initial thought was that the podium would not protect him—please, someone get there to protect him. Please let no one be hurt. It never once occurred to me that I might be one of them.

I was frozen, still staring at the president seconds later, when we heard a second round of four shots. By then, President Trump was surrounded by a sea of navy-blue: at least a half dozen Secret Service agents formed a protective shield around him.

From the huddle, I could hear a female agent say, "What are we doing? What are we doing?" Then, "Where are we going . . ." and the sound of her voice was muffled.

Michael shouted as the second four shots went off: "Those were gunshots!" He tackled Shannon to the ground and dropped on top of her. The next thing I knew, I was knocked off my feet and shoved to the ground by lead Trump press advance man, Michel Picard III. Hovering over me, he held me down, his knees pressed against my shins. My face landed in the dirt and gravel, and the rest of my body covered my daughter.

"Are you okay? Are you okay?" Picard shouted at the three of us. Then he lowered his voice and took a deep breath. I could hear him slowly exhale to regain control.

"Stay down. I got you. Stay still, stay calm," Picard said. His voice was soothing, but his hands told a different story; he was shaking hard. I watched him look down at his hands as he tried to stifle the adrenaline.

I was still just feet away from the president. From my vantage point, I could see the huddle of blue suits surrounding him; I saw his bloody face between the gaggle of men and women around him. An agent said, "Go around to the spare, go around to the spare . . . hold, hold, when you're ready, on two."

Or maybe he said, "When you're ready, on you." I wasn't sure.

Time seemed to stop. Everything that was happening around me occurred in slow motion. The crowd, eerily, was not screaming, not really. In fact, it sounded like they were still cheering. On the ground, with gravel digging into my legs and arms, I could hear only one woman screaming. Her screams were primal—I don't know if she was hurt, if someone she loved was hurt, or if the trauma was too much for her. It seemed like she was moving around in the stands behind me, moving toward something that was across from me.

Her screams were gut wrenching.

One or two of the last four shots sounded like they came from a different-caliber gun.

I could hear President Trump talking back and forth with members of his detail, who were still tightly circling him. At least three male voices were talking. One said, "Ready. Move up."

A different one said, "Go, go, go!"

But they remained crouched down. Another agent said, "Hawkeye's here, moving to the spare."

"Spare, get ready. Spare, get ready," said the agent who, from my vantage point, seemed to be the lead.

At least two, maybe three of the agents then shouted, "Shooter's down. Shooter's down—are we good to move?"

A male voice answered, "Shooter's down. We're good to move."

A female agent asked, "Are we clear?"

Someone said yes, they were clear, and to move. Their protective circle became mobile as they stood up with Trump, keeping a circle around him. I heard Trump say, "Let me get my shoes, let me get my shoes."

An agent said something like, "I got you, sir," and Trump said again, "Let me get my shoes on."

I could see Trump's silhouette, and it looked like he was trying to put on his shoes, which one of the agents had knocked off. An agent told him, "Hold on, sir, your head is bloody."

Trump was insistent. "Let me get my shoes."

A female agent relented. "Okay."

As they slowly started to move, I heard Trump say, "USA! USA! USA!"

The detail raised him to face the crowd. He lifted his fist, pumping the air: "Fight. Fight. Fight." His voice was raspy. The crowd erupted in joy and relief.

An agent urged, "We got to move, we got to move."

They exited the stage, and I saw him raise his fist again three times. The crowd was now shouting "USA! USA!" as he and the agents headed toward where I was lying on the ground. A Secret Service agent in full camouflage crouched over me, looking into my eyes, and aimed his AR-style rifle directly at me as the president made his way toward me. The agent and I exchanged glances, but I was oddly not afraid.

Trump and all the agents moved past me. I could barely see his face, but I saw enough to notice the blood running down his cheek. Picard hadn't moved. He was still on top of me, in a protective stance, and I could feel his knee digging into my calf. I thought, *That's going to leave a mark.* Shannon and Michael were still underneath us.

Shannon and I both tried to take photos, but Picard and Michael were having none of it. "We don't know if there is another shooter," Picard said firmly, so we didn't move.

Trump did not have his MAGA (Make America Great Again) hat on as they moved him past me. I saw his hat fall at some point while they were huddling. An agent miraculously grabbed the hat before it touched the ground and was still holding onto it while holding onto the former president.

The hat's rescue was short-lived. When the group passed us, the hat slowly fell, landing in the gravel by my face.

I turned just enough to see past the loudspeaker that was behind us and watched the agents help Trump get into a vehicle, which they then surrounded. The motorcade paused for a moment, and then he was gone.

I thought back to the early morning. None of what had been planned that day had the three of us in the buffer zone by the president. I let out what I thought was going to be a deep sigh, but it somehow turned into that kind of little laugh you have when your day has gone haywire.

Shannon said, "Are you okay?"

I laughed just a little bit again; it felt like the only release I had in me at that moment. "Yeah, I'm okay. Remember when the thing I was most worried about this morning was getting here on time?"

"Yeah, I remember," Michael said. "It almost cost me a beef jerky."

––––––

The morning started thirty-six miles away at my home in Westmoreland County, Pennsylvania. It was only 6:09 a.m., but the sun was already streaming through my kitchen window and the temperature was inching toward 79 degrees Fahrenheit. I checked the weather for the day and saw that the temperature was forecast to peak in the late afternoon at 93 degrees. There wasn't a cloud in the sky.

Not ideal conditions for a day I would be spending with Shannon and Michael and about fifty thousand other people, standing in a treeless field that for seventy-five years had been home to the Butler Farm Show. We would be in the sun for hours, waiting for former President Trump to hold his first big western Pennsylvania rally of the 2024 election cycle.

I was scheduled to interview Trump that day. Shannon is a photo-journalist, and my son-in-law was coming along to carry the tripod and lighting so that she and I could stay somewhat presentable for the interview.

Shannon and I had agonized the night before about what we could wear that would be proper for a presidential interview but also not leave us drenched in sweat. In the end, we were dressed properly and drenched in sweat a half hour after we got there.

Chris LaCivita, one of Trump's campaign managers, told me earlier in the week that I would get five to seven minutes with Trump before the rally started. *That's fine*, I thought. I had inter-viewed Trump before, and "five to seven minutes" with him usually meant twenty minutes. He loves to talk.

That thought reminded me to double-check that I had my notepad with my top three questions I wanted to ask him:

FIRST: Mr. President, there are thousands of people out there waiting to see you. If you win in November, what will you say to them four years from now that you were able to deliver to them after winning the presidency?

SECOND: What was going through your mind during your debate with President Biden as he faltered over and over again?

AND THIRD: If Biden were pressured by his party to drop out, what approach, if any, would be different if you find yourself running against Kamala Harris?

I stuffed the notebook in my purse. They weren't the kind of ques-tions that got the clicks newspapers crave, including my boss, but I was looking for the answers that voters were seeking.

I wasn't nervous about the interview. I had interviewed Trump several times before. The most famous interview was a freelance job I did for the *Atlantic* in September 2016 at a Marcellus Shale event in Pittsburgh, when I said to him, "Voters take you seriously but not literally, whereas my profession takes you literally but does not take your candidacy seriously."

That interview happened several days after I had accepted a buyout offer from my longtime job at the *Pittsburgh Tribune Review*. I had to knock on several doors of major newspapers before the *Atlantic* agreed to hire me.

I had also interviewed the president at different rallies across the country, including one in nearby Erie and at the White House. We had always conducted a good back and forth in our conversations. And besides, interviews rarely rattle me. I had been interviewing presidents on both sides of the aisle, or those who were running for the White House, for decades. It's just what I do.

What I *was* nervous about, though, were the logistics of this day. Really nervous.

My greatest anxiety is always: Will I get to the event in time? With a Trump rally, you have to factor in large crowds, parking challenges, and long lines to get to the facility.

The rules are strict about what time the press can enter as well as the cutoff time for access to the event. You have to print out a press parking pass and then remember to bring it with you.

I looked down at the confirmation email. Despite having read and reread it several times, I noticed for the first time that I was supposed to bring a press ID card as well as a government ID. Well, despite working for the *Washington Examiner* for eight years, I had no press pass; the paper doesn't issue them. I panicked. Logistics, ugh. I frantically called Picard, who assured me I would be fine.

Shannon and Michael have four children—Eleanora, Milo, Louisa, and Rocco—ranging in age from eight to one. They live just over the hill from me, and my grandchildren are as rambunctious and active as my kids were while growing up. They are my everything, so much so that rarely does a day go by when I do not see them. However, getting someone to watch four children, who may not be used to watching four children, for an assignment that would likely last at least twelve hours, was a task.

At one point the night before, my daughter called me, near tears, saying she just couldn't find someone to watch the kids. I told her if that was the case, I wasn't going either. Pretty bold choice on my part, to be honest. Luckily, I didn't have to follow through because, at the last minute, Michael's parents, Mike and Debbie Venditti, were able to watch them all day. They had called in the cavalry of his brothers and their wives to help. As I said, my grandkids are my everything, but they are also a lot to handle.

The media credentials said we had to be there at 2:00 p.m. I lied to my daughter and son-in-law, telling them we had to be there at one o'clock. Why? Because Michael is never ready on time. And, as predicted, when I arrived at 10:30 a.m., fifteen minutes before we were supposed to leave, my son-in-law was washing the car and clearly had not yet showered.

Outwardly, I smiled and hugged him. Inside, I felt the worst anxiety rush through me, something that I would feel all day. Thank God I had the wherewithal to put that one-hour buffer in our schedule. Shannon was ready to go, and she got all four children ready while we waited for Michael to take his shower.

When I am anxious, I pace. My son Glenn calls it house trotting. The pacing got a little out of control, although we left only fifteen minutes later than planned.

The drive to Butler from Westmoreland County is just over an hour and twenty minutes without Trump traffic. Just after we exited the Pennsylvania Turnpike, we hit the county line at noon.

Google Maps showed at least another hour to get to the Butler Farm Complex—all of that delay because of the Trump traffic jam ahead to get into the parking lot at the farm complex.

Michael decided to pull over at a Sheetz gas station to get beef jerky because he was hungry.

"Michael!" Shannon and I screamed in unified exasperation.

"I promise—time me, I'll be thirty seconds," he said. My anxiety worsened, and Shannon looked anxious too. He sprinted out of the Jeep and, to his great credit, returned in under a minute with three giant bags of beef jerky.

"Want some?" he asked with a broad smile, clearly proud of his accomplishment. Honestly, if I hadn't been so filled with anxiety at that moment, I would have congratulated him. Instead, we both screamed, "Michael, let's go!"

Within a mile or two after pulling away from the Sheetz lot, the decorated cars, trucks, and motorcycles started appearing on Route 8. They were in front of us, passing us, pulling over to pick up snacks. Probably beef jerky. A line of about thirty motorcycles with massive "Trump 2024" signs fluttering in the wind were pulled over to the side. There were oversized trucks with American flags billowing from their tailgates. There was not one but two vans with a shrink-wrapped image of Trump covering the entire vehicle. A limo passed us with an American flag shrink-wrapped around it. It seemed like every car along the highway was decorated, creating a sea of red, white, and blue for the next twenty miles.

As we approached the two-mile-long residential stretch of well-kept homes and manicured lawns—houses built from the turn of the twentieth century to midcentury—that leads to Buttermilk Road, the final road that would take us to the parking lot, there were three homes in a row with children outside courting rally-goers with lemonade stands.

With the mercury already at 93 degrees, plenty of cars pulled over to grab a red SOLO cup of lemonade, delighting the children who were trying to make a buck. There were also some fairly enterprising adults with tricked-out barbeque stands, and the sweet smell of campfires, savory meat, and spices filled the air, enticing even more people to pull over.

There was even a moonshine stand, with a guy playing a fiddle beside the still. I shouted out the window to get their number—I needed to follow up with those guys.

As we got within a mile of the Farm Show Complex, some enterprising homeowners were sitting on chairs in their yards, holding signs offering parking spots on their property for a price; the closer you got, the more expensive the cost.

A mile away, it was $10, and by the time we were just a quarter mile away, people were paying $40 for the convenience of not having to wait to park at the official lot or having to wait in the parking lot once the rally was over.

Plenty of people took these residents up on the offer. Hundreds of people were walking along Buttermilk Road, carrying folding chairs and water bottles as we slowly inched our way toward the parking lot.

As soon as we got to the parking area, we asked the state trooper where the press parking lot was and showed him our parking pass. Of course, I had obsessively asked my daughter to print out three "just in case." Shannon glanced at the clock—"Oh my God, Mom, it's almost 1 o'clock and we still have to park and get to the press entrance."

For once, she panicked and I did not. I looked at her and sheepishly admitted, "Um, the cutoff time is 2, not 1." She rolled her eyes, but before she could say anything, I interjected, "What? You guys are always late."

"Fair enough," she said, and we all laughed. But I still wasn't relaxed yet. We did have to get to the press entrance, allow security to sweep our gear, and then go through the magnetometers—it's at least a half-mile walk. I made sure, three times, that everyone had their driver's licenses, and then we started walking toward the mags.

The security check was uneventful, and we headed over the rise of the hill, where we could finally see the stage and the vendors along the way.

Neither Shannon nor Michael had been to a Trump rally before. I watched their reactions as their senses were almost overwhelmed with sounds and smells. It is hard to capture in words, to properly express the emotions of the people who attend these rallies. They can become so tangible that they make everything around you feel big.

There is a real sense of people who feel like they are part of something bigger than themselves—and part of something that connects them to each other. It's a very different description than most reporters would give. But most of them didn't grow up in places like Butler, where my family originally settled in the 1790s. Most mainstream media reporters don't know people like those who attend these rallies. It's foreign to them, and they often describe them in their stories as "strange," "weird," "uneducated," "far-right," or "left behind."

"Everyone is so happy," Shannon said. She pulled out her Nikon and started photographing everything—*click, click, click.* She turned to capture people buying trinkets at a vendor's booth, and two very muscular Black men, standing in the middle of the grass and holding up bawdy T-shirts that read "Fuck Joe Biden," smiled and posed for her.

A little kid holding a tiny American flag and his grandmother's hand caught Shannon's eye. *Click, click, click.*

Michael saw Scott Presler, the young, relentless social media advocate for signing people up to vote, known for his long brown hair and, more importantly, for going across the country, and specifically across Pennsylvania, to register voters for the Republican Party.

Presler was standing in his register-to-vote booth, signing people up. Yes, there were people attending a Trump rally who had not done that yet. With him was Slippery Rock mayor Jondavid (J. D.) Longo, a former marine who governs a small college town on the edge of Butler County.

Presler gave me a hug. Michael was a bit awestruck. "Wait, you know Scott Presler?"

It made Presler laugh. "Wait, you know Salena Zito?" Michael got a selfie with him.

We found the entrance to the press riser and Picard, and we made our way toward the tables and chairs that had been set up. They were all hot to the touch; nonetheless, we tried to sit down. The sun was beating down relentlessly. I let out a deep sigh, and my daughter and Michael laughed, knowing that now I could relax: we had accomplished the hard part of getting here on time and getting into the press area.

The rest of the day would be fine.

Thankfully, the Trump advance team had placed water bottle stations all over the massive farm field behind the stage area because the heat was merciless and we still had hours to wait before the rally began. People were cresting the hill, and slowly the stage area, with risers on all sides, began to fill up.

Picard pulled me over to a shady area for the photographers who cover Trump. "Okay, here is what I am told. You have five minutes with the president. I will come and grab you and Shannon and Mike ten minutes before he is to go on stage, and we'll do the interview," he said.

I conveyed that to Shannon and Michael, and Picard asked whether they wanted to go into the buffer area with the press pool. They both wanted to, but Shannon wanted to be there more. Since only one of them could go, Michael relented and Shannon joined the press pool.

"Okay, I will grab you before the interview, place you in there, and then grab you afterward," Picard explained.

We watched the people make their way down to the field. I interviewed Harry Norman, a Vietnam War veteran who had served three tours of duty and twenty years in the military. He uses a cane now, but dang if he wasn't dressed to the T in a navy shirt and khaki pants, and holding a tiny American flag. At seventy, he's still not retired from farming. Norman said he was overwhelmed with emotion to be there.

"I've never been to a political rally in my life," he said. I offered him water, but he declined and made his way toward the stage.

The crowd started to swell. People were walking toward the stage area with newly purchased Trump flags, hats, sipping cups, and Pittsburgh Steelers Terrible Towels, as well as funnel cakes, hot dogs, and french fries smothered in cheese.

Matt Popovich, eleven, was beaming as he walked past me carrying a sign that read "Kids for Trump." I asked him and his dad, Mark, if this was his first Trump rally. "Yeah," Matt said with a smile. "But it's not going to be my last."

It was now 3:38 p.m., and Picard pulled me aside again. "There has been a change in plans." I immediately thought, *There it is; it's canceled.*

All that planning for naught. Well, that was just what I got for lying to Shannon and Michael about what time we should be there. God was definitely punishing me. What am I going to tell my editor? Honestly, it is amazing the things you can think of in a split second.

"You are now going to interview President Trump after the rally," Picard said. "They are running late."

The one thing that every seasoned journalist knows for certain is that when plans or schedules for an interview change, the likelihood that the interview will happen decreases.

"We can't change that?" I asked Picard. But I knew his answer before he said no.

Shannon and Michael were visibly annoyed, mostly because they knew this meant we would get home much later than we planned and they had the kids to think of. They decided to take a walk around the vendor booths. "Don't go too far," I warned. And Shannon rolled her eyes again. "Mom, we are going to be here for another, what, seven hours?"

I immediately texted LaCivita: "Hey Chris. The plans just changed with our interview and I am making sure that this thing is really going to happen. Like, I know how this goes. First it's moved and then it doesn't happen."

I sounded kind of bitchy, which is not my thing, but it was hot and I had other people to think about besides myself.

LaCivita immediately texted back, "No. No. No. All is good. No changes with the interview. It is happening. We are just running late."

I started feeling anxious again. I looked around and realized that the crowds of people had filled not just the stage area but also the whole area beside the risers and as far as the eye could see. Every space was filled with people, and they looked hot. I watched as several local reporters, including me, grabbed cases of water from the press cage to haul over to the gates.

"Pass them back into the crowd," I shouted. The exercise took my mind off the worry that everything about the interview might go south. I texted my daughter to come back because now I was worried they wouldn't get back to the press entrance through the massive crowd.

Twenty minutes later, Susie Wiles, Trump's campaign manager, texted me: "President Trump thinks that five minutes after the rally is too short for an interview," she wrote. There it is. I knew it. I was about to tell Shannon it wasn't going to happen when Susie texted more: "He would really like it if you and your photographers would fly from Butler to Bedminster so you could do a full interview. We'll have someone drive you back after the interview."

Well, that took a turn I did not see coming.

I looked over at Shannon and Michael. There was no way they'd agree to do this. No way Michael's parents would watch the kids overnight. I resigned myself, even before I asked them, to the fact that I would unfortunately be doing this solo.

"Wait, what? Say that again?" was Shannon's response. "How is this my life?" To my utter surprise, they were all in. You have to understand, Shannon has done assignments with me before but never anything with such high stakes.

And Michael, who works in the venture capital world, navigates deals, not this crazy political world.

Now it was time to get Michael's parents to agree. Debbie answered Shannon's call quickly but hedged when asked; she was apprehensive about their safety on the plane with Trump, with so many people in the world hating him.

It is important to note that Debbie and her husband Mike are about the biggest Trump supporters you could find, so this apprehension had nothing to do with their politics. She is just a natural worrier.

Debbie consulted her husband and her brother, Perry Bruno, who was with them at the house. Perry told her, "My God, Debbie, it is a chance of a lifetime. Tell them to go."

Shannon assured her, "This is the safest place in the world we can be. He is the most protected person in the world."

The realization of what was going to happen sunk in, and Shannon asked, "How are you so calm? We are going on the plane with the former president and going to Bedminster . . ." Her voice trailed off.

I reminded her that all she had to do was capture some great photos.

Picard came over seconds later to tell me about the change in plans, and I reacted as if I didn't already know. He looked at me and said, "Who are you, exactly?" I just shrugged.

By then, there was nothing but a sea of people filling up the farm field. Weeks later, one of the board members of the Butler Farm Show told me there were at least fifty thousand people there that day, using the same metric they use to measure their annual farm show in July. I had no doubt that was the truth.

By 5:30 p.m., a half hour after Trump was supposed to arrive, his motorcade caught the attention of everyone in the top row of the bleachers. He was here. The news traveled fast, and the crowd erupted in applause. The countdown of his music playlist told me it would be at least another half hour before we'd see him.

Picard grabbed Shannon for the buffer area where she was to join Doug Mills from the *New York Times*, Evan Vucci of the Associated Press, and Anna Moneymaker of Getty Images. Michael and I waited at the press riser. Within minutes, Picard was running toward us.

"It's 'go time,'" he said. "Let's go now."

I looked at Michael. "I guess the plans have changed and we are interviewing Trump before the rally," I said.

As a reporter, it is part of the deal to always be prepared for things to change—and they sure had changed several times that day. Michael and I weaved our way through a tiny buffer that was carved out with metal fencing, making our way through the crowd to where Shannon and the other photographers were waiting to go into the buffer zone. Picard grabbed Shannon: "Go time!" he told her.

She looked at me, and I shrugged. "I guess we are doing the interview now," I said.

Jondavid Longo, mayor of Slippery Rock, and Rico Elmore, chair of the Beaver County Republican Party, were both walking out as we were rushing in. Inside the first curtained-off section were several young families, at least two dozen first responders, state troopers, and firefighters, all waiting in line to meet the president.

Picard said, "Come on, let's go!"

I was confused. "Where are we doing the interview? We need to set up the lighting."

Picard seemed equally confused about where the interview would happen. "Stay here. I'll be right back." He walked into the second curtained area. A wave of delightfully frigid air whiffed from behind the curtain.

I turned to Shannon. "Well, now we know why he stays so cool when he gets out there on stage. He brings his own air conditioner." Shannon didn't laugh. She was busy trying to get all of her equipment ready for whatever split second we would have with Trump in the next few minutes.

Picard emerged from the curtained-off room where Trump was greeting people. He smiled. "You are not interviewing him right now. He just wants to say hi. You are still going to Bedminster."

Shannon and Michael laughed. "Okay, Mom, this I gotta see."

Now, I had not seen Trump in person since 2020 when I interviewed him in Latrobe, Pennsylvania, weeks before that year's election. In February 2023, he got sore with me for interviewing

Florida governor Ron DeSantis—so sore that he wrote a Truth Social post calling me "FAKE NEWS REPORTER SALENA ZITO" because I had interviewed someone who was then considered his biggest potential rival for the Republican primary process.

Even though my story never mentioned that DeSantis was running, Trump was pissed at me. You have to remember, at that time, Trump was not at the top of the Republican primary polls and voters were still raw from losing several midterm US Senate races they believed Republicans would have won had Trump not pushed for candidates like Dr. Mehmet Oz in Pennsylvania and Herschel Walker in Georgia over more traditional Republicans in those states' primary races.

Trump's turning point in the voters' hearts did not begin until one week after my DeSantis interview when he showed up forty-two miles from the Butler Farm Complex in East Palestine, Ohio, where a Norfolk Southern freight train had derailed, spilling hazardous materials. It was a day filled with horrors, sleet, and mud. Trump, wearing galoshes, handed out McDonald's hamburgers and cases of water. It was then that his fortunes began to change with voters.

I received a call from him one day out of the blue in May of 2024. It came in as a restricted number, a call I would rarely pick up, but I was watching my grandchildren at the time and impulsively did pick up. To my great surprise, Trump was on the line.

I chased the kids running around in the yard and tried to keep them occupied as we talked. Trump laughed when he heard me trying to keep them from doing whatever siblings do to each other when the caregiver is on the phone. We talked about Pennsylvania. At the end of the call, Trump said, "Sometimes people around me think they control everyone I talk to. Here is my cell

number. Within reason, call me any time, and please don't share
my number."

And that was that. It was not the first president's cell phone number I had been given. I still have Barack Obama's and Joe Biden's.
At one time, I had Bill Clinton's and Hillary Clinton's cell numbers.
I've never called any of them. I guess that is who I am now, I thought
that day, the keeper of presidential cell phone numbers.

Now Picard said the president wanted to see me. Before I even
made my way into the wonderfully air-conditioned room, I heard
that familiar voice: "Saleeeeena," he said, exaggerating the middle
of my name. "You look great. You lost weight. My goodness, look
at her hair, everyone—doesn't she have the best hair in journalism?
Possibly in America."

It was hard not to laugh. Also, it was hard not to be embar-
rassed. Everyone in the room, mostly police officers and senior
staff, was looking at me. At least, it felt like that. I really don't like
the attention and found myself wishing I could crawl behind a
chair. He came in for a hug. Not a big deal to me; I hug everyone
and everyone hugs me. Even Hillary hugged me in my old news-
room at the *Pittsburgh Tribune Review*. So did Obama in New
Hampshire.

"Salena, it's so great to see you. How are you doing? How are
all those grandkids?"

Trump always remembers my grandkids. "I love my grandkids
too," he said. "I love being around them."

It was just before six o'clock. "I am really looking forward to
our interview," he said. Inside the tent with me were about forty
local cops—men and women. As I left, I heard him telling them,
"Thank you so much for your service."

He was in great spirits. At rallies like these, he always is.

Picard took me, Shannon, and Michael to the buffer area. "May as well as stay here rather than go back to the riser," he said. "We'll be leaving as soon as the rally is over. Take photos, videos, whatever you like. Make sure you end up toward the end over by the speaker."

Within seconds, the voice of country music singer Lee Greenwood blared through the speakers: "God Bless the USA."

Trump appeared on a red-carpeted walkway in his trademark blue suit and MAGA hat, waving to supporters as the excitement grew to a frenzy. He strode to the podium.

The applause seemed to last forever. It was about 6:05 p.m.—I know that because I looked at my watch when Trump started to speak. To his right was a screen that, in the lead-up to the rally, showed videos of the president urging people to vote in person or by mail, and also showed several videos of him speaking directly to the crowd.

Now a large chart about illegal immigration appeared on the screen.[1] Trump proceeded to do two things I have rarely seen him do: go full Ross Perot and use a chart at a rally and turn his face and neck away from people at a rally.

Trump rallies involve a give-and-take between him and the rally-goers; he feeds off of them as much as they feed off of him. So although he may turn to face another section of the crowd, he rarely takes his gaze away from them.

Yet, at this moment, he did those two things at the same time, actions that he had never done before, and they saved his life.

Had he not decided to use that chart to underscore his remarks about how illegal crossings at the southern US border had dipped during his presidency, and had he not turned away from his supporters to glance at the chart, one of the shots fired at 6:11 p.m. likely would have hit the base of his skull and killed him.

Chapter 2

Middle of Somewhere, Butler, Pennsylvania

The county of Butler grew out of the county of Allegheny seven years after the end of the Revolutionary War. The bucolic region along the sloping foothills of the Appalachian Mountains was named for a man who never lived here, Richard Butler, an industrious Irish immigrant who served this country before it was a country, nearly losing his life several times on the battlefield in that pursuit.

The Pennsylvania regiment that Butler commanded was one of three that had joined forces with the French army under the Marquis de Lafayette; Butler was the first American officer to greet the French when they landed near Williamsburg, Virginia.

Their first combined battle proved to be the turning point of the war when Lord Cornwallis was forced to surrender after a successful siege of his army at Yorktown, Virginia.

David, my great-grandfather times four (representing the McJunkin side of my family) moved to what is now the city of

Butler in 1796 after emigrating from Ireland to Plum, Pennsylvania, with his parents at the end of the Revolutionary War.

At the age of eighteen, David moved to Butler and bought four hundred acres of land. Within a year, he had courted and married Elizabeth Moore and, wanting to impress his in-laws and new bride, he prepared a simple marriage supper of cornbread baked on a stone hearth by the fireplace.

Within a few more years, he became one of the largest farmers in the county.

Initially, he engaged in the business of distilling whiskey; however, according to his journal, his religious convictions caused him to rethink that enterprising side hustle and to instead erect one of the earliest and most extensive saddle tanneries in the area.

In 1830, when he purchased a saw and grist mill, iron furnace, forge, and foundry in the small Butler County town of Slippery Rock, he set the stage for generations of descendants of skilled artisans who passed down his love of working with his hands.

David served as a soldier in the War of 1812 and was remembered as a pioneer in this county long after his passing in 1840. David had a son, Archibald, who married Hannah, and they had a son, George. After George married Priscilla Newman in 1875, they had six children, including my great-grandmother Mary McJunkin, who married John Eyster of East Palestine, Ohio.

Eyster fancied himself a thespian. How do I know that? Well, I inherited his collection of William Shakespeare's works, and written on the inside cover page of each edition, in perfect penmanship, was *John Eyster, Thespian*.

In reality, he was a coal miner and farmer with a calling to serve his community. He ran for state representative in East Palestine, just over the state line, as a Free Silver Democrat the same year William Jennings Bryan ran for president. Both lost. My great-grandfather earned only twelve votes, and Bryan, a few more.

Eyster had better luck as a nonaffiliated candidate when he moved to the next town over the hill, New Waterford, Ohio. There, he served as mayor of the small village for twenty-two years. His wife Mary, my great-grandmother and an enterprising McJunkin, owned and ran a general store along Bull Creek in the center of town. One of their four children was my grandmother, Mildred.

New Waterford was never much of a town. There was a diner, my great-grandmother's store, the upholstery factory that sat across the street from my grandparents' modest farm, and three churches. Mildred wanted more, so she left small-town life at seventeen to go to the big city of Pittsburgh for nursing school. When she left, she was engaged to a local boy; when she came home for a visit a few summers later, she broke off the engagement and later married my grandfather, Henry Peiffer, whose family had roots in—you guessed it—Butler.

Henry had been in the news industry all his life, forced into it at age twelve when his father Clifford, also a newsman, made above-the-fold, front-page news by jumping off what was then called the Sandusky Street Bridge. Henry immediately started work as a copyboy for the *Pittsburgh Sun-Telegraph*.

Henry spent as much time as he could at his aunt's farm in Butler, both as a child and a young man. He went hunting and fishing and worked chores on the farm. As a young man, Henry had a vaudeville act that he performed in his spare time with his sister Katherine.

He and Mildred had three children, one of whom is my mother, Joan Arden Peiffer. My grandmother named her after Joan Crawford (Arden had been the storied actress's original stage name).

Mildred didn't look like other grandmothers. She was glamorous, with perfectly finger-waved black hair and blue eyes. She wore pencil skirts and pearls. Even as a child, I found her beautiful, until multiple sclerosis took that away.

My mother, a devout Lutheran, met a boy at the same high school I would attend at age fourteen. He was the captain of the Perry High School football team, and she was the captain of the cheerleaders. In 1950, they danced to Elvis's music at sock hops and fell in love. When both turned twenty-one, my mother did the unthinkable and married my brown-skinned, very Italian, devout Catholic father Ronald, who hailed from a loud immigrant Italian family.

To say that our family is rooted to the dirt under our feet in western Pennsylvania is an understatement—two-hundred-plus years in the same three-county region will do that to you. Then again, almost everyone who lives here has similar roots. Most families who call places like Butler home, whether they have been here for one generation or nine generations, share stories of hard work, perseverance, failure, troubles, loss, and hope, all intertwined in their families' lore.

Former Allegheny County executive Rich Fitzgerald used to say that eight out of ten people in the region live within eight miles of where they grew up—it is a rootedness that has held for generations. A recent study from researchers at the US Census Bureau and Harvard University found that 60 percent of young adults (the study measured people at age twenty-six) live within ten miles of where they grew up. Eighty percent of young people live within one hundred miles.[1]

Drive along Connoquenessing Creek, which parallels South Main Street, and you'll think the view of the city of Butler could have been drawn by Norman Rockwell, all the way down to the sign that reads: "The City of Butler. A great place to live."

Talk to most people in Butler, young or old, blue-collar or well-to-do, and you will discover that they have a sense of connection with one another, with the land, and with a way of life that has remained constant for generations. For decades, my family has come here to camp and fish. The people who live here work hard, play hard, and want their children's lives to be better than theirs, though they still want them to live close enough to come over for family dinners on Sundays.

Located thirty-five miles north of Pittsburgh, Butler depended on more than agriculture to become what it is today. During the 1870s, oil boom towns were built throughout the county, towns that still exist today—such as Petrolia and Karns City—and flourished within months of the discovery of oil.

However, even the most optimistic prospectors never believed those towns would be permanent. They were right, and by 1880, Butler's fortunes in the oil industry had mostly faded.

Despite this, the city of Butler had already begun to emerge as a bustling business district. The steel and manufacturing robber-barons of the late nineteenth century, who amassed their fortunes from railroads, steel, and other manufacturing, began to settle in Butler. So did a variety of ethnic immigrants who worked for them.

It was here that Jeep was born, an invention of the American Bantam Car Company, which developed the vehicle in 1940 in response to a request from the US Army to 134 tractor and auto manufacturers to design a four-wheel-drive, 40-horsepower 1,300-pound reconnaissance vehicle that could haul soldiers as well as heavy equipment.

Oh, and the company had to do that in forty-nine days.

Bantam met the moment—even made nearly three thousand Jeeps for the army—but eventually lost the contract because the company could not produce the required seventy-five vehicles a day. The army gave its blueprints to Ford Motor Company, and Bantam never produced another vehicle again.

Butler still celebrates the Jeep, though, with a yearly festival to mark the city's place in history, featuring local bands and long rows of tents with food vendors. Here, you can go off-roading in your Jeep.

As a family that owns five Jeeps among us, we rarely miss this festival. It's the kind of thing that defines Butler: honoring tradition through a cultural touchstone, even one that didn't quite make it big.

Throughout World War II, America's men and women didn't just serve in the military. Those who could not instead supplied the steel and rail cars needed for the troops overseas.

Butler was also the home of industry giants who brought a new kind of prosperity to the city at the end of the nineteenth century, like the Pullman Standard railcar facility that used to sit just outside the city limits and employed, directly or indirectly, most of the city's adults.

The men who worked at the facility known colloquially as the "wheel works" made steel railcar wheels for Pullman Standard for over 150 years. The company not only employed much of the town; it also funneled millions of dollars into the Butler economy, money that paved roads, improved schools, and helped to support local charities.

When war threatened the country, according to data compiled by the Butler Historical Society and the Pennsylvania Historical Society, the employees of Pullman Standard manufactured more than seven million artillery shells and bombs, in addition to railcars, for American and Allied forces in World War II.[2]

Postwar, Pullman Standard employed four thousand people in both the factory and offices. The company's closure in 1980 nearly destroyed the community's hope, prosperity, and purpose.

The historical society notes a *Butler Eagle* article, dated February 17, 1982, in which then-mayor Fred Vero estimated a $60 million loss to the county from Pullman Standard's closure. School districts lost significant portions of their budgets; suppliers and contractors laid off employees.

A June 20, 1982, *Butler Eagle* article reported that Butler's unemployment rate skyrocketed to 17.5 percent practically overnight.[3] Pullman's demise was a direct result of changing American habits, and the residents of Butler were the collateral damage of that change. People no longer flocked to passenger trains for transportation; they used cars.

Today at the same location sits Butler Works, part of Cleveland-Cliffs Inc., a steel producer. What today's employees produce is essential to American life: transformers for electrical grids on which America depends for reliable, affordable energy.

Butler Works is the largest industrial employer left in the city of Butler.

In March 2024, the Biden-Harris administration came within a hair of killing the local plant in reaction to pressure from the Sierra Club and other heavily bankrolled and powerful "climate justice" entities such as the Natural Resources Defense Council, which sued the Department of Energy (DOE) for not properly doing its customary six-year review of energy efficiency standards.

That lawsuit might have placed the final nail in the coffin for Butler, had Pennsylvania governor Josh Shapiro not stepped in to halt the DOE rule.

In the 1960s, all of the counties surrounding Butler County began to lose population—except for the city of Butler, the county did not lose population—largely because of what began to happen in a sleepy agricultural village that had no proper business district. People in the city of Pittsburgh wanted to move out, but not too far out, and Butler County's Cranberry Township became their destination.

Between 1960 and 1980, the population of Cranberry soared from 1,045 to 22,000. Today, it sits at more than 32,000, and the township employs more than 21,000 people in over 1,000 businesses, including a major medical facility. Butler County's property tax is lower than neighboring Allegheny County's, and the township's school district is well regarded. Home values in Cranberry range from $500,000 to more than $1 million.

Despite that rich history and newfound affluence at the county line, Butler County rarely has been a place where candidates for US president have campaigned to ask people for their votes.

Only two candidates—Democratic presidential nominee John F. Kennedy in 1960 and Republican nominee Donald J. Trump in 2020 and 2024—have done so. In fact, Trump is the only sitting US president to visit the county in its 224-year history.

Yes, James Buchanan and James Garfield came, but that was well before they had even considered running for president. William Howard Taft came as well, long after he had been president.

When Trump announced in October 2020 that he would be holding a rally here, I remember that it triggered some confusion among Democrats, Republicans, political strategists, and members of the news media.

Why in God's name was he going to Butler?

My reaction was different. Very different. To me, the decision was brilliant, largely because of what I noted earlier: the importance of a sense of place. I often write about "place" in politics because place matters. However, most Democrats and Republicans who make their living in Washington, DC, rarely get that. If they did, their candidates would win more often.

What is "place"? Rootedness.

And, for that matter, most reporters would better understand what and whom to cover in today's politics and, more importantly, where to cover events if they understood the importance of place. By definition, a successful reporter in today's Washington- and New York–centric American journalism is placeless. These reporters cover politics with a worldview that comes from a lack of rootedness. It is not necessarily a bad thing, but it is restrictive in that they often do not understand the people they cover in politics—why they think the way they do and do the things they do. Many reporters do not understand why never leaving one's hometown is not viewed as a bad thing and instead is honored as an achievement by family and peers. They do not understand the value of living close enough to your family to have supper together on Sundays, something that those who are rooted typically do.

And they don't know how to cover these voters because they don't know anyone like them in their own social circles.

Reporters often write about the contrast between coastal elites and the country's "fly-over" areas, but the difference is more complicated. The dichotomy isn't necessarily rural versus urban, or low-density versus high-density areas of America, as Tom Maraffa, professor emeritus of geography at Youngstown State University, once told me. The difference is more between the "placed" and "placeless." In short, people who are rooted in their places versus people who are essentially nomads, like reporters and politicos who flock to Washington and New York not just to make a living but also to form policy or political messages.

These professionals—placeless people who share no affinity for rootedness to their hometowns—are often highly critical of fly-over folks and develop an affinity for ideology and abstractions as opposed to neighborhoods and cities.

As I noted in a story I wrote for the *Washington Examiner* in 2018 about the placed and the placeless, the lives of the coastal elites, academics, big-business owners, high-tech innovators, entertainers, and media personalities—those I call our cultural curators—have led to this lack of affinity because they are so mobile.

People who live in Butler are generally not so mobile. It's not because they are stuck; their lack of mobility, or their desire to live in their hometown near family, friends, and traditions, is purposeful.

People in small towns, rural areas, and affluent areas of Butler have been tied to their places for generations. This is why issues such as climate change and globalization are fundamentally viewed differently, including among the college-educated in Butler.

The placeless think of global policies, abstract efficiencies, and lofty ideas like social justice. The placed think of how things will affect their neighborhood, town, or city.

Maraffa told me, "People who voted for Trump share a rootedness in place. Think of people in J. D. Vance's *Hillbilly Elegy* or the TV series *Justified*, which was tied by the phrase 'We dug coal together,' an expression of place."

So when Trump decided to hold a rally in Butler, the placeless in the media and a lot of "very smart" people in the Republican and Democratic Parties did not recognize the importance of place in American politics.

What they missed was that Butler is many things to many people—and people all over the country would see themselves in that rally—bucolic, industrious, suburban, and historic, filled with rolling hills of farmland, a college town, a roaring steel mill, and that all-important outpost of suburban Pittsburghers who brought with them prosperity and commerce.

Why come here? Butler is reliably Republican. It isn't going to swing the election and would not swing an election cycle. But for practical purposes, it makes sense: Butler has an airport, it's located within the media markets of both Pittsburgh and Erie County, another important place for politics, and it is situated just over the state line with Ohio.

It is the nuance that is missed, though, and it is both complicated and important: Butler matters because it represents so much more than Butler. There are people across the country who are much the same, people who work with their hands, work the land, and even work in C-suites. Perhaps they could make more money elsewhere, but they decided to stay near their hometown because they were tied to the region and that had more value to them than money.

Because those who value place are skeptical toward certain policies, they're often accused of ignorance, racism, and denialism—all lazy tropes that reporters or Democrats use because they would never dream of thinking about how the policies they champion affect their places.

Trump's 2020 event was held on Halloween night at Pittsburgh-Butler Regional Airport, and the number of people who attended was unprecedented. The best way to describe the line of cars waiting to get into the rally is to visualize the scene at the end of the movie *Field of Dreams*, where hundreds of cars approach the field, fulfilling the prophecy that people will come to watch baseball.

The crowd was the largest Trump would draw.

Three days later, he would lose the state and the election—and then things would get really dark.

Two years later, Trump would return to Pennsylvania to campaign for Mehmet Oz, his handpicked candidate for US Senate, a decision that divided Republicans. When Trump declared his intention to run again in 2024, the response to the announcement lacked the spectacle to which he was accustomed.

A few days after Trump's announcement, Oz lost his Senate race to Democrat John Fetterman. Other candidates Trump had endorsed in Republican primaries, including Herschel Walker in Georgia, Blake Masters in Arizona, and Adam Laxalt in Nevada also lost, and Republicans began to sour on the former president.

His popularity dropped in the polls while that of Florida governor Ron DeSantis rose. DeSantis had scored a historic win in Florida that November, not only for himself but also for candidates down ballot, with wins for Republicans in districts and seats the party had never won before. As a result, the Republican electorate shifted its attention to DeSantis.

Trump responded to that shift by taking swipes at the Florida governor almost daily on social media, calling DeSantis "DeSanctimonious." By January of 2023, the esteemed New Hampshire University poll showed Trump was garnering only 30 percent of the New Hampshire electorate vote to DeSantis's 42 percent in the country's first primary state.

Trump had never been so far down in the eyes of the Republican primary voter. Many were still trying to recover from the events of January 6, 2021, still bruised about losing the US Senate majority in the midterm elections a few months earlier, and they just wanted a winner to lead their party.

Trump was sharing so many personal grievances, he reminded voters of the celebration of Festivus from the 1997 *Seinfeld* episode "The Strike." According to the sitcom, Festivus is a day when everyone has a chance to air their grievances. But for Trump, Festivus was starting to become a daily occurrence.

Within twenty-three days of that New Hampshire University poll, Trump began to claw his way back into the hearts of Republican voters by showing up at a little village forty-two miles from

Butler on a day filled with unforgiving rain and sleet. On February 3, 2023, a Norfolk Southern train derailed in East Palestine, Ohio, spilling vinyl chloride and butyl acrylate. Despite the gloomy weather and concern about hazardous chemicals still lurking in the air and mud, Trump showed up at East Palestine when President Joe Biden didn't.

Few noticed. I call it his inflection point. I am not sure that even he knew it at the time, but I sure did as I watched hundreds of folks line up along Main Street as his motorcade, filled with state and local law enforcement officers, siren-ed its way into town.

With him was the young US Senator J. D. Vance who had been sworn into office less than a month earlier.

Young and old, male and female, Democrats and Republicans, and even the traditionally crowd-shy Amish families all stood in the icy rain as Trump drove into town only a couple of weeks after that thirty-eight-car train dumped poisonous residue into the water, soil, and air. It was a chain of events that began with a fiery derailment, the immediate effects of which continued for two days, followed by a controlled burn that released hydrogen chloride and phosgene into the air and water.

Within a month, the shift toward Trump in the polls had begun, but on that day, I wrote in my rain-smudged reporter's notebook: "If he is able to resurrect the magic of 2016, understanding the forgotten man and woman and the dignity of work, it started here, the day he showed up when Biden refused."

Trump understood that everyone's lives there had changed on February 3; he understood the significance of weeks of silence from the White House regarding people's concerns. *Newsweek* reported searching through 380 messages released from the White House press pool from the date of the crash to the day Trump arrived in

East Palestine and found no direct statements from Biden on the community. Someone had to tell these people that he "saw" them and understood their fear and anger and pain.

Of note, Biden tweeted about East Palestine the day before, when Trump announced he would be coming to the Columbiana County village. Four days after Trump's visit, when pressed, Biden said he had no plans to show up.

"You are not forgotten," Trump said at a news conference, flanked by cases of "Trump" bottled water that he had brought for residents of the community. With him were Ohio's senator Vance, East Palestine's mayor Trent Conaway, and other local elected officials.

He looked at the audience and said, "In too many cases, your goodness and perseverance were met with indifference and betrayal."

Trump then walked through the village wearing a long overcoat, his trousers tucked into Carhartt boots, and talked with people about how the train derailment had changed their lives and likely those of generations to come.

One resident, Tami Tsai, told me nearly a year later when I noted what I had observed in February of 2023 when Trump showed up, "In a lot of ways, we are the symbol or poster child of the kind of place Washington forgets. President Biden underscored that by not coming then or now or ever."[4] (Biden did not go to East Palestine until February 16, 2024.)

Tsai added that unless someone "experienced what we did, unless you understood what it is like to be discarded as not important enough, Trump showing up for us showed he cared. There will always be people who said it was a stunt. Well, he didn't have to do it, but he did. That is more than I can say for President Biden."

Trump's visit reminded people that he was physically there for them at a time when they were hurt and worried. He told them, "I am ready to fight for you."

It's a phrase he would use seventeen months later when he returned to Butler for his first rally since the one held in October of 2020. He and his campaign chose a location that's a tiny dot on a folded paper map with a stretch of blue lines, a place where presidents from either side of the aisle rarely visit.

When Trump rolled up on July 13, 2024, it was just two weeks after his debate with President Biden, a performance by the sitting president that shocked many Americans, including those in the press, because it revealed that the eighty-one-year-old was struggling cognitively. His party began working furiously to unite to push him out of the White House race.

Butler, a county unfamiliar to many, one that few visited if they didn't live there, was about to change everything in a way that no one saw coming.

Chapter 3

The Hand of God

BUTLER, *Pennsylvania*

We were lying on the ground for what seemed like forever after the Secret Service had taken Donald Trump away from the farm show grounds to Butler Memorial Hospital. Shannon and Michael were still partially underneath me, and Michel Picard, the Secret Service agent, was still crouched over us.

When Trump's motorcade pulled away, I heard two distinct sounds behind me: people in the crowd shouting, "We love you, Trump!" and a frantic cry, "Medic! Medic! Medic!"

Several people, including law enforcement officers and first responders, formed a scrum around someone who had been sitting in the stands behind Trump's podium. Even from my position on the ground, I could see them quickly carrying away a limp figure: a man with a dark towel over his head. I saw Rico Elmore, who just a short while ago had given an inspiring speech before Trump took the stage, his white shirt smeared with blood.

There was a man I didn't know, older, distinguished, who reminded me of Burt Lancaster's character in the 1989 film *Field of Dreams*: Moonlight Graham. His hair was silver, and he wore a white T-shirt with "USA" printed across the front and a "Make America Great Again" hat tilted to the side. He, too, was smeared with blood as he walked down the aluminum stands. A few women near him walked down too, and as they turned to leave, I could see blood streaked across the back of their calves.

"Get in the tent, get in the tent," a Secret Service agent shouted. We scrambled to get up, and Picard swiftly ushered Doug Mills, Evan Vucci, Anna Moneymaker, Shannon, Michael, and myself past the stands and toward the tent where, just moments earlier, Trump had been talking to me about my grandchildren and going to Bedminster with him.

Picard stopped midway along the stage while he listened to instructions through his earpiece. I looked over at the podium. It was tilted, and I thought, Trump would not like that. His Diet Coke can was lying on the platform along with a stained white rag an agent must have used to stem the bleeding from Trump's ear.

The Diet Coke reminded me of my interview with Trump in the West Wing seven years earlier. His staff had stacked Diet Cokes for him near the Resolute desk. Funny, the things you think of at the oddest times.

"We are going to go back in the OSA," Picard said. I had no idea what that meant. Honestly, there are so many acronyms in government-speak and campaign-speak that I really can't keep up with them. We all quietly followed him.

———

As the chants of "USA!" and "We love you, Trump!" faded, the crowd began to exit. There was no panicked crush of bodies, which you might expect at such a time. People just started heading toward the farm fields where their cars were parked. Cheeky flags that vendors had erected billowed in the breeze, and there wasn't a cloud in the sky. At any other time, a moment like this would feel almost dreamlike, the rural scenery on a beautiful summer evening. It wasn't that different from the cloudless blue-sky weather on September 11, 2001, I recalled. This early evening had no business being quite so beautiful.

We spent at least an hour in the tent. Moneymaker was crying—not sobbing, just letting the tears flow the way they do when you've been part of something traumatic. We hugged.

"Are you okay?" I asked. Anna shrugged as if she wasn't sure how she felt. I understood; I felt that way too. I hugged Mills, the photojournalist who was with President George W. Bush on 9/11.

Grace, a member of Trump's press team, sat on a folding chair. The last time I saw her she was directly under the podium while he was speaking, making sure the photojournalists in the buffer zone were able to get good photos of him. She, too, was weeping, but more dramatically. Tears streamed down her face, and she struggled to catch her breath. I found an unopened bottle of water lying on the ground in the tent and told her to close her eyes, take some deep breaths, and then sip the water.

Shannon and Michael were texting family members to let them know we were okay. I began to pace the enclosed area and tried to peek out of the curtain to see what was happening outside. I'm not sure what I expected—probably chaos and fear, so the somewhat silent movement of tens of thousands of people out of the stands toward the parking areas was somewhat comforting.

Picard came over and asked me to move away from the opening in the curtain. I looked at my phone for the first time: the number of unread texts was in the hundreds. How the heck can I ever respond to all of these? Oddly, my son Glenn, who was camping in the Rockies and had no cell service, and my eighty-seven-year-old parents, who were at a friend's birthday party where an Elvis impersonator was busy entertaining the guests, would go straight to bed once home.

None of them would find out until a day later what had happened.

───────

After an hour, the Secret Service allowed Mills, Vucci, Money-maker, Shannon, Michael, and me to leave the tent. Stepping outside into the sunlight was jolting. The massive American flag that had been held up by two cranes was blowing in a slight breeze. Under it, behind the stage where Trump had been shot, stood about two dozen Pennsylvania state troopers and what looked to be an equal number of local police officers. They resembled stone sentinels, guarding the area; few of them talked or moved around. Then one of them told me they were waiting for instructions from the feds and asked us politely to move along.

Past them was an empty field. The last time I had looked back on that field was when Picard had ushered us from the press riser to the stage to see Trump, and I remembered thinking, *This crowd has to be one of the largest of his I've personally seen*, and I was worried about how spending hours in the heat would affect people.

Now there was no sound except for the wind whipping the slightly worn flag and the occasional crunch of water bottles under our feet as we made our way back to our Jeep.

Along with discarded water bottles scattered on the field, there was an abandoned wheelchair. An American flag had fallen from the back of it; my daughter picked it up and planted it in the ground in front of the chair.

Our calm, almost peaceful quarter-mile walk toward the parking lot added to the confusion of trying to process what had happened. We reached the area where the vendors had been selling flags, T-shirts, patriotic paraphernalia, hot dogs, funnel cakes, and hoagies. Now they were taking down their tents, moving kitchen equipment, and folding up tables.

Everyone worked quietly. Retired Army Ranger Sean Parnell, who also spoke before Trump's speech, appeared to be comforting the few stragglers left in this area. He told us that one person had died, and two other people were gravely injured.

We crested the hill and saw the parking lot still filled with cars even though most people had exited the rally field more than an hour ago. Despite the trauma, the overbearing heat, and the long wait, people weren't blowing their horns. I saw no disputes, no anger—in fact, we found people eager to help each other.

Tom, whose last name now escapes me, was in his truck with his wife, his elderly mother-in-law, and her sister. He asked if we happened to have any water. Shannon grabbed four bottles from a cooler in the back of our Jeep and ran them over to him.

"Any beer in there?" Tom joked. His family shared a bag of pretzels with another family with three hungry kids in a van behind his truck.

"Where you guys from?" Tom asked us. Within minutes, we learned that his mother went to high school with my parents, and my son-in-law is somehow related to Tom's brother-in-law. Shannon and I got out of the Jeep and started walking around the field. We heard similar conversations across the parking area among people in vehicles. I heard Shannon's camera shutter click as she took dozens of photos.

"No one will ever believe this happened," Shannon noted. She was right. It was a story no reporter would mention, despite scores of them being there. Maybe they didn't get it. Maybe they didn't understand the rootedness that makes people want to connect with each other during a tragic moment. It was soothing to witness in the aftermath of the shooting—an inspiration to be our best selves.

It was another hour before law enforcement officers allowed the cars to exit. I wrote two stories on the way home, both partially dictated, for the *Washington Examiner* and the Free Press. Michael and Shannon live less than a mile from me, and when we got home, I did several cable news hits, then quickly fell into a deep sleep, never hearing the dinging notifications of texts that flooded my phone all night.

———

"Good morning, Salena! It's Donald Trump. I wanted to see if you and your daughter Shannon and Michael are okay. And I wanted to apologize that we weren't able to do the interview."

I wasn't quite sure how to respond to that. I had known that he was okay from the chatter in the holding area after the shooting, but I wasn't expecting a call from him. So I did something I rarely do in a casual conversation, let alone when talking to a former president. I cussed like a truck driver.

"All due respect, Mr. President, but are you fucking kidding me? You've just been shot; I was only near you!" I blurted out, then immediately regretted it. I apologized, thinking of how my parents would not be happy.

He laughed. "Seriously, Salena, are you and your family okay?" he asked, clearly needing an answer.

I assured him we were fine, that I had spoken with both my daughter and Michael just an hour earlier and none of us felt rattled. All three of us were amazed that we weren't feeling what we expected, but we agreed that someday it would hit us, just not now.

The conversation lasted twelve minutes. Trump marveled that there had been no panicked stampede. He was deeply saddened by the death of Corey Comperatore, a fifty-year-old firefighter attending the rally, and he worried about the other two men who had been shot. He was impressed with the treatment he received at Butler Memorial, and he recalled vividly the moment he was shot—and that several of the events that happened before the shooting were out of the ordinary for him.

"The funny thing, when I bring that chart up, I always do it at the end of my speech, but I started talking a little about immigration. I said, 'Bring the chart up now. Can you get it now?'" he said.

Trump explained that when he turned to point to the chart, he felt the whisk of wind as something came at him. His first thought was that he got whacked by a mosquito.

"And I said to myself, it's either a giant mosquito, the greatest mosquito in history, or that's a bullet," Trump said he thought when he grabbed his ear. In a split second, he realized that it was indeed a bullet, and he ducked down, immediately surrounded by agents. "When I came up—they actually thought I was gone—so when I came up, they were happy when I put that hand up."

He questioned out loud, more to himself than to me, why he had decided to change everything on stage: Why didn't he wait until the end of the rally to talk about the chart? Why did he turn his head ninety degrees? He repeated the question several times.

Neither of us directly answered it in this first phone call.

"You know, if I had just done things the way I always do, the way I planned to, that bullet would have struck between both ears, not just whacking one ear."

He told me he had been stunned by the number of people—who he admitted he would usually call "radical left-wing lunatics"—who had reached out to make sure he was okay.

"I'm getting calls from Democrats that are unbelievable, from different people you would never think would call me . . ." His voice trailed off.

"This could be an opportunity to bring the country together," he said.

He called me seven more times that day, each call lasting around ten minutes. In each one, he expressed the same struggle to figure out why he did what he did that day, impulsive decisions that in retrospect saved his life.

We talked about God, divine intervention, and Trump's purpose, but the meaning hadn't yet crystallized. I gave him room to figure it out. Not every reporter would do that, I suppose. Maybe it was the wrong decision, but it felt right in the moment to not press someone who had just been shot, likely because I was just as out of sorts as he was.

Trump's last call came toward evening, after he had gone back and forth with his team, his family, and the Secret Service, and they had decided to stick with the plan to fly from his resort in Bedminster, New Jersey, to Milwaukee, where the Republican National Convention was set to begin the next day.

I could hear him talking to people, and it was clear they were walking. He explained they were about to board his plane for Wisconsin. One person with him was Sen. Lindsey Graham of South Carolina, and Trump handed the phone to him for a moment to say hello, then quickly grabbed it back.

I said, if it was okay with him, I wanted to write about how he felt; so I asked him again—this time more pointedly—whether he thought that a higher power had a hand in his making out-of-the-ordinary choices to impulsively pull up the chart when he did and turn away from the crowd to point at it.

Trump paused. "God," he said. "The hand of God."

He added that he thinks the hand of God has been there many times, but he was sure he never thought about it when it happened. "I got impeached twice, the endless court cases, so when

I think about it, while none of that compares to what happened yesterday, I cannot dismiss that God has been with me. This time, though, it was a big one," he said.

I asked him if this was a sign to do something different from regular politics.

"So, I am giving a speech on Thursday," Trump said of his planned speech at the Republican National Committee (RNC) Convention in four days. "I had a humdinger—this was one of the greats. Had this not happened, this would've been one of the most incredible speeches." He paused for a moment. "Honestly, Salena, it is going to be a whole different speech now. It's changed."

I said nothing. I could tell he was processing things. Then I heard several voices as people joined him on the plane and gathered around him. In the background, I heard Graham's surprised reaction to Trump's next proclamation: he had ripped up his original speech and would start from scratch.

"Lindsey, it is changed," he said. "My speech has totally changed. It went from the world's most vicious speech to 'Let's bring the country together.' May not be as exciting, but there it is."

Trump told me the plane was about to take off, and he asked, "Are you coming to Milwaukee? We can continue the interview there." I told him no. My original plan had been to cover the convention from the road in Pennsylvania, and I wanted to stick to that.

"Okay," he said. "See you on the road?"

"See you on the road, sir."

Chapter 4

Shattered

The First Twenty-Four Hours in Pennsylvania

BETHEL PARK, Pennsylvania

On the day after the attempted assassination of Donald Trump and the murder of father, husband, and retired fire captain Corey Comperatore of Sarver, Pennsylvania, several dozen reporters stood beside the yellow caution tape strung along Highland Road in the middle-class suburban Pittsburgh community of Bethel Park. Little movement came from the driveways of homes lining the street. People kept their curtains closed. Daily life in the normally quiet Milford Drive neighborhood had been shattered a day before at the campaign rally just over forty miles north of Bethel Park.

Matthew and Mary Crooks own a modest red-brick home located a few houses beyond the caution tape along Milford Drive. A law enforcement sniper killed their twenty-year-old son Thomas with a single bullet wound to the head at 6:25 p.m. the day before while he was lying on the slanted roof of the American Glass

Research (AGR) International building just outside of the Butler Farm Show Complex grounds.

At 6:06 p.m., Thomas Crooks ripped off four shots toward the main stage where Trump was speaking. The candidate had just turned ever so slightly to his right, and one bullet grazed his right ear. Another bullet mortally wounded Comperatore, and the other two shots gravely wounded spectators David Dutch, a fifty-seven-year-old US Marine veteran from New Kensington, Pennsylvania, and James Copenhaver, seventy-four, of Moon Township, Pennsylvania.

Crooks's rooftop position was located only four hundred feet from where Trump stood. We later learned that the Bethel Park man had been waiting at the Farm Show Complex for hours.

Initially, police blocked Milford Drive to residents for a few hours, beginning on the evening of July 13. One woman said authorities had evacuated her from her home in the middle of the night. The events shook her in the way I imagine happens to people who yearn for a simple, quiet life—the comforts of home, the familiarity of daily routines, a sense of safety in one's home and belongings—and she was looking for someone or something to ease her stress. Her hands shook despite the heat of the day. She didn't give her name.

The police told reporters that they had evacuated people while they searched for a possible bomb in the Crooks's home. Reporters were later told that along with the AR-style rifle found beside Crooks's body, law enforcement officers also found a cell phone and remote transmitter. Two explosive devices, a drone, a tactical vest, and four magazines of ammunition were found in Crooks's car near the Farm Show Complex. The FBI confirmed all of this six weeks later.[1]

Milford Drive looks like the type of street you'd find in many bedroom communities in western Pennsylvania—the street dips up and down as it follows the sloping terrain, and the sidewalk is crisscrossed with cracks from the pressure of tree roots, the tilting road, and the wear that heavy winter snows, torrential spring rains, and oppressive summer heat can have on concrete. The mostly brick single-family homes are a mix of post–World War II split levels and ranches with well-kept yards.

Like much of suburban America, this is the kind of place where people know each other and call out hellos from their yards or the street. At one time, these neighbors might have held block parties on summer weekends or holidays and exchanged cookies at Christmastime. On this day, however, Jerry, who lives a block away and gave me only his first name, mourned the way society had changed from when he and his family first moved to the neighborhood in the late 1970s.

"We have gone from a neighborhood of front porches and kids playing in the streets to backyard decks, closed front doors, and people keeping to themselves," said the father of a grown son. "I don't think that is unique to here, and I don't think it is necessarily good. We are too isolated—parents and kids have their heads down in phones and games. It is a step forward every day to losing our humanity when we don't interact and see people as living beings."

According to county tax records, the Crooks family purchased their home in 1998 for $87,000. The Allegheny County Real Estate website lists the home as a three-bedroom, one-bath red-brick ranch in fair condition. The house was built in 1950, one year after Bethel Park's incorporation as a borough, as young couples migrated to the suburbs from the city of Pittsburgh, swelling the town's population from 11,000 to 24,000 in less than ten years.

The Crooks family came here during the second wave of new homeowners, a generation about to live out the American dream by owning their first home. Many were the children of those belonging to the Greatest Generation—Americans born between 1901 and 1927. Mary Frizzi Crooks's father, John Frizzi, was a first lieutenant in the US Army during the Vietnam War and a member of American Legion Post #290. When Frizzi died in 2010, his obituary noted his great love for his grandchildren, one of whom was six-year-old Thomas Crooks.[2]

For the most part, Bethel Park has remained a middle-to-upper-class neighborhood, with homes not quite as pricey as neighboring Mount Lebanon and Upper Saint Clair, which bookend the municipality, but there are million-dollar homes with swimming pools, artfully landscaped yards, and a few backyard pickleball courts spread throughout the community.

The school district attracts many families who shop at the South Hills Village mall and other nearby shopping districts, including a Whole Foods store and boutique jewelry and clothing stores. Both local medical centers, the University of Pittsburgh Medical Center and Allegheny Health Network, have state-of-the-art outpatient medical facilities nearby.

This is one of the few Pittsburgh suburbs with trolley service into the city, including a loop from downtown to PNC Park and Acrisure Stadium, the respective homes of the Pittsburgh Pirates and Pittsburgh Steelers. And like many city and suburban school districts, high school football rules on Friday nights in Bethel Park, and soccer fields are filled with youngsters on Saturdays and Sundays.

Yet on this day, after the fateful Trump rally in Butler, people were stunned by what happened—and that it involved someone from their community. Those at the local Dunkin' expressed disbe-lief that it had happened, as did those who knew Thomas Crooks. Young and old, people shook their heads as they talked about the shooting, acknowledging that it had shattered their sense of calm.

Who was Thomas Crooks? For those who didn't know him, and perhaps some who did, the answer emerged slowly—painfully so—with gaps of missing information still apparent months later, so that we may never truly know him or what motivated his actions. Oddly, Crooks had no social media presence. His politics seemed unformed; police said he registered as a Republican when he turned eighteen but donated to the Progressive Turnout Proj-ect, a Democratic Party–aligned political action committee.

Thomas Crooks and his parents largely kept to themselves, said neighbors who rarely saw them. Did they know them? No, most people said, or perhaps "barely."

Matthew and Mary Crooks have been licensed professional counselors for twenty years, according to state licensing records. He is a registered Libertarian, and she is a registered Democrat. Father and son were members of a local gun club.

Bethel Park has a fair mix of Republicans and Democrats. It used to be that the wealthier enclaves around Pittsburgh leaned Republican, and Democrats dominated the more middle-class neighborhoods, but that has changed as both parties have changed. Nonetheless, this borough has almost always been equally mixed. In 2020, Trump won Bethel Park by sixty-five votes, which under-scores just how even-handed things are here.

Crooks graduated from Bethel Park High School in 2022 after spending twelve years in the school district with roughly the same kids for all his formative years. His classmates were dumbfounded when they heard the news. Yes, he was quiet, they said. Sure, he did not have a core group of friends with whom he hung out, but he was the kind of kid who kept to himself.

As it did to many kids of Crooks's generation, COVID-19 interrupted nearly two years of his teenage life. The pandemic kept students out of schools for months in 2020, and remote learning continued even after that, so Crooks missed much of the educational and social opportunities students typically have in their sophomore and junior years.

A few weeks after the attempted assassination, Kevin Rojek, the FBI's Pittsburgh Field Office special agent-in-charge, told reporters that authorities had no evidence that Crooks had any help with his plan that day, nor did they find any indication that he had mental health issues.

"We are working hard to determine the sequence of events related to the subject and his movement in the hours, days, and weeks prior to the shooting," Rojek said a month after the rally.[3]

————

To the outside world, Crooks had disappeared into the abyss of self-isolation. Beyond social media, he had no social presence, period. Kids who had taken the school bus with him for years recalled little interaction with him.

He attended the community college. He joined the gun club, but that didn't raise red flags in western Pennsylvania, where owning a gun for hunting is a way of life for many. The Pennsylvania Game Commission reported selling 2,657,245 hunting licenses statewide in 2023. Gun ownership for self-protection is also a western Pennsylvania tradition; in the same reporting period, there were 1,650,034 active licenses to carry a gun in the state.

Crooks's apparent loneliness and determination to do something sinister seem to have begun almost a year earlier, in August

2023, when he joined the Clairton Sportsmen's Club to develop his shooting skills.

Among the things that stand out to me was this: He spent most holidays at the club, practicing and practicing his shooting—not holidays like the Fourth of July or Labor Day, but Christmas and Valentine's Day, days that are meant to be spent with loved ones or someone special. Instead, records show he was at the gun club.

Clairton Sportsmen's Club is nestled in the hills of the Monongahela Valley and is spread over 180 acres, across the boroughs of West Mifflin and Jefferson Hills. Records provided to news organizations by Senator Chuck Grassley (R-IA) showed Crooks visiting the club and logging on to practice over forty times in the eleven months before the Butler shooting, spending more than 80 percent of his time on rifle practice. The club has several rifle ranges, including one that is two hundred yards—Crooks was less than 150 yards from the stage in Butler.

He made his last visit to the range at 2:45 p.m. on Friday, July 12, the day before the rally.

BUTLER, *Pennsylvania*

On the morning after the shooting, Governor Josh Shapiro made his way to the Butler County Farm Show grounds.

In a phone conversation, Shapiro explained to me that he had received the call mere minutes after Trump had been shot and immediately began receiving updates on the situation from local, state, and federal law enforcement officials.

"Anytime an emergency occurs, you want to make sure that operationally you understand what's needed. And so, my first call is to my chief of staff. Obviously, we were in regular communication with state police and others on the ground. You just always want to make sure in an emergency you're addressing the operational needs," he said.

His first concern was Trump's condition. "Once it is confirmed he is okay and the president has left the area and received medical treatment, and by his own statement said he was fine, we were really just focused on any individuals there who may have been harmed. Obviously, we now know it was two people who were critically wounded and one whose life was cut short," Shapiro said.

He paused. A father of four children, Shapiro knew he had to make a truly difficult phone call to a family that had just lost their father. So, he hesitated, first calling the local dignitaries he knew had been there. "I spoke to several Republicans who were there, members of Congress, even [Senate candidate] Dave McCormick," he said.

He did not call Trump.

"Candidly," he said, "not for any other reason than I really did not know how—and I'm not trying to be so glib, I really did not know how to reach him."

Within seven days, Shapiro would become a leading contender to be Kamala Harris's vice-presidential running mate on the Democratic ticket and, briefly, possibly even the presidential nominee. President Joe Biden announced the following Sunday that he would end his bid for reelection because of lingering fallout from his disastrous debate performance with Trump on June 27. Many in his party were concerned about the eighty-one-year-old's ability to continue to run for office.

Shapiro said his focus in the hours after the shooting, with his team back in Harrisburg, was how best to communicate the shock and sorrow, the anger and fear that he knew so many people were feeling—in Butler and elsewhere.

"It was very important to me that I be there on the ground today, that I have the opportunity to go to where the shooting occurred," he said.

Shapiro spent the morning walking the grounds at the Farm Show Complex, talking with people who work there. He received a briefing from the FBI, state police, and other federal agencies investigating the events, and then he made his phone call to the Comperatore family.

They gave him permission to talk about Corey to reporters.

"Corey was a 'girl dad,'" Shapiro said of the man who dove on top of family members to protect them from gunfire at the rally. "Corey was a firefighter. Corey went to church every Sunday. Corey loved his community. And most especially, Corey loved his family.

"Corey died a hero," the governor added.

Somewhere in this moment, Corey Comperatore became a symbol of the "everyman" in America, the kind of person many know in their everyday lives. Perhaps you went to school with a guy like Corey or helped coach your kids' softball and soccer teams with someone like him. He was one of those guys who would volunteer to help you move, fix your porch, or just show up when you needed help. A man of honor with a deep love for his family and community, he was part of the force in American politics that's often unseen and that few understand.

After a news conference, Shapiro told me he thought it was important to speak about the issues that he believed mattered most to folks and to "not allow anyone to forget that this was a tragedy that came to a wonderful rural community in Pennsylvania, and that we lost a fellow Pennsylvanian—and two others needed our prayers to be able to get through their darkest hours."

Speaking as "we," a term that he often uses to express inclusion and commonality, Shapiro added, "We felt that it was a moment that required some moral clarity from the governor of that state."

Less than twelve hours before, the pasture spreading in front of Shapiro held tens of thousands of his constituents, gathered for what should have been a festive rally, wearing patriotic-themed clothing and eating funnel cakes and sandwiches smothered in french fries and gooey cheese. Now the area was littered with hastily dropped folding chairs, plastic water bottles, and even a wheelchair.

How much had changed in such a short time.

"Obviously, what was going on there is not my politics," Shapiro said. "I disagree with former president Trump on many things, but the first thing I thought was that there were Pennsylvanians here who were genuinely excited, not only to hear from the former president but that he chose their community to come to.

"There is a point of pride here, and the people who visited this farm show to hear him speak, they didn't deserve to have to deal with, in the case of three individuals, bullets shattering their bodies, or in the case of others, the trauma that came along with this shooting."

Shapiro won the vote of many Trump supporters in 2022 because he embraced the importance of showing up in places like Butler. Just four months earlier, Shapiro saved the iconic Butler Works steel plant, owned by Cleveland-Cliffs, which the Biden administration was about to put out of business with its climate-change regulations. He had received a hero's welcome when he came to the plant to make the announcement.

In 2022, voters here recognized Shapiro's ability to connect with them, giving the Democrat 43 percent of the vote, far outstripping the less than 35 percent that his fellow Democrat, Joe Biden, had won against Trump in 2020.

Back-of-the-napkin calculations tell you there had to be a few thousand Trump-Shapiro voters attending the rally, showcasing that while both men are wildly different in their politics and comportment, they each understand the importance voters put to feeling "seen" and respecting their sense of place.

"I think meeting people where they are matters," Shapiro nodded in agreement when I mentioned this. "Understanding their hopes and their fears, their minds, the things that frustrate them, the things that excite them—and it makes me a better governor being in their community, listening to them, and then being able to take the lessons I learned there back to the Capitol to make new laws, advance new policies, and get shit done."

SARVER, Pennsylvania

The sun was starting to set. The drive along North Pike Road from the Butler Farm Show Complex to the Buffalo Township Volunteer Fire Company was pastoral and golden as the light dimmed to twilight.

I was not sure what I would find upon arrival, but what I did find nearly brought me to tears.

The three oversized garage doors at the fire department were open. The headlights and alarm lights, all a brilliant red, were lit up on the three fire trucks facing outward in the garage. Overhead, on a sign that read BUFFALO TOWNSHIP VFC, firefighters had draped black fabric. A neon-yellow firefighter's helmet hung on the left pillar of the first garage and directly below it was a jacket with BUFFALO emblazoned across the top in reflective yellow tape and COMPERATORE below it. An axe, a pair of boots, and a single bouquet of white roses, with one pink rose in the middle, were arranged beneath.

The small town was already honoring Corey Comperatore the best way they knew how, with an outpouring of love for a man who had been a project and tolling engineer, had served his country in the Army Reserve, and had spent years as a volunteer firefighter.

His funeral service was held here a few days later. A fire truck with a massive flag billowing in the wind from its ladder led a procession of hundreds of other trucks on the way to the service. The lead fire truck carried Comperatore's flag-draped casket to Cabot Methodist Church.

A sharpshooter team was stationed on a nearby rooftop, another reminder of the senseless reason that we were there.

Some families lined up in their driveways as the procession made its way down Winfield Road. Some people held flags; others held their hands in prayer. Some onlookers raised their hands in salute.

The moment was overwhelming yet peaceful.

Just one day earlier, Corey Comperatore's jacket and helmet were displayed at the center of the stage during Trump's speech to the RNC in Milwaukee. Americans waited to hear what he would say in his first public address after being shot—it was an image and a speech that intimately and emotionally intertwined the everyman, Butler, and the candidate in a complicated context that perhaps few outside the heartland could comprehend.

Chapter 5

A Front Row Seat

MILWAUKEE, Wisconsin

Erin Koper took a deep breath.

The forty-three-year-old western Pennsylvania native was about to step out onto the same stage where, in two days, former President Donald Trump would formally accept the Republican Party's nomination for another term in the White House. It was day two of the Republican National Convention, prime time, and she had a story to tell about how crime had upended life in her hometown of Pittsburgh that she hoped would resonate with everyone watching.

It was a story and perspective she hoped would make a difference in the election. A story Trump and his campaign advisers Susie Wiles and Chris LaCivita, a Pittsburgh native, had a hunch would.

The theme of the night was "Make America Safe Once Again," and the event was designed to showcase regular people, as well as a gallery of Republican luminaries, delivering a central message of restoring law and order in our nation as well as taking a stand for law enforcement.

The night before, Erin sat in the same hall she was about to address and watched Trump make his first public appearance forty-eight hours after surviving an attempted assassination. She could feel the hall roar as delegates and attendees went wild with cheers when he was shown standing backstage on the stage screen. When he stepped out onstage, his face was flushed with emotion as Lee Greenwood sang "God Bless the USA."

Trump did not address the convention that night, nor would he this night, but his presence was felt everywhere: from sitting in his seat in the hall to people watching his granddaughter crawl up on his lap to his decision to have Erin and other ordinary people like her speak at the convention.

Just hours earlier, Erin had watched from the green room as the delegates nominated Trump to lead their ticket for a third time and welcomed J. D. Vance, the young new Ohio senator, as his running mate.

Now it was her turn to address the same hall, the same country, the same president.

Waiting in the green room, Erin watched as Rep. Elise Stefanik of New York, the then House Republican conference chair; Rep. Steve Scalise of Louisiana, the House majority leader; Speaker of the House Mike Johnson; one-time primary rival turned Trump confidant Vivek Ramaswamy; former ambassador to the United Nations Nikki Haley; and Florida governor Ron DeSantis took their turns leaving the green room to speak.

Erin sees Trump walk into the hall and blurts out, "He's here" much louder than she intended, and everyone in the green room starts laughing. She knew she would be speaking in front of him, but things just got real. Senator Tom Cotton (R-AR) and Governor Sarah Huckabee are both in the room with Erin; it is Huckabee who calms and inspires her. Huckabee tells her they are all nervous and encourages her to put a smile on her face and give them hell.

DeSantis steps out to speak. Erin is up next.

No pressure at all.

As DeSantis is ending his speech, Erin feels the adrenaline surge of her heart pounding throughout her body just before her name is called. She feels warm all over. She takes a sliver of a moment to quietly chuckle to herself at the absurdity of this moment. How was it that she of all people was about to face not just everyone in attendance at Fiserv Forum for the second night of the convention but also the entire country tuning in to watch?

And in that audience was President Donald Trump, who, just like her, was in Butler just days before.

How did *she* get *here*, she thought as she walked out onto the stage and into the glare of the bright lights.

Erin's father, John Brown, was born into poverty in Armagh, Northern Ireland, in 1934. John's mother, Maureen, was only sixteen when he was born, so the raising of John Brown went to his grandparents Julia and Barney Toal, who adopted him and cared for him. When he reached eighth grade, it was decided that John was finished with schooling, and he went to work on a nearby farm.

It wasn't that hard work wasn't for him. It was. He had a knack for carpentry. For fixing things. But John Brown wanted more. He saved what money he could from his farm work and fled the family homestead in the middle of the night. The determined youngster traveled over 138 miles from Armagh to the Collins Barracks in Dublin; he lied about his age and joined the Irish Army.

It was the beginning of the era of "the Troubles," a conflict over the status of Northern Ireland that pitted Protestants and Catholics against each other. The stigma of being a Catholic from Northern Ireland was too much for the young man, so he left for England. It was there that he fell in love with and married Maureen Witstanley. She was eighteen, a coal miner's daughter who had to raise her younger siblings since the age of ten when her mother died. John was twenty-four. They had two children, Colleen and Terrance, and soon wanted a better life for their family.

The working-class conditions in 1960s England were uneven; housing was substandard, access to health care was difficult if not impossible, and there was an insurmountable ability to improve one's situation. The family turned their hopes toward America.

In February of 1960, John, Maureen, eighteen-month-old Colleen, and one-month-old Terrance landed on the shores of the United States and made their way to Weirton, West Virginia, for a better life. The couple had four more children: Michael, Christina, Matthew, and Erin.

John's idea of living the American dream came true through hard work. A naturally talented carpenter, he found work with the City of Weirton, eventually making his way to building inspector for the city and then director of public works. The municipal building where he worked was located across the street from St. Paul's Catholic Church where Erin attended school. She often visited him after class.

Erin grew up in a very tight-knit family and community; everyone in her family and in Weirton was Catholic and a Democrat. The town was just over thirty miles from downtown Pittsburgh, and everyone Erin knew back then worked in some capacity for Weirton Steel, once the largest employer in West Virginia as well as the state's largest taxpayer.

Until April 2024, Weirton Steel remained the world's largest tin plate producer. Then the US International Trade Commission rescinded tariffs on tin imports from China, sealing the fate of the once-mighty plant that gave western Pennsylvania and West Virginia communities hundreds of thousands of jobs for over one hundred years.

Erin met her husband Jacob Koper while in high school. They reconnected after she came home from college; she was the only child her parents had managed to put through school. Jacob, handy like Erin's father, had gone to the local trade school. She was twenty-five; he was twenty-two. They moved to Pittsburgh and married ten years later at St. Mary's on Mount Washington. Erin shed her journalism degree after her side career as a makeup artist took off; Jacob began his own construction business.

Erin's politics were the same ones she had learned from her parents, New Deal Democrats. Her father was very involved with the local Democratic Party in Weirton and ran for local council office several times as a Democrat. He never won, but it never deterred him from trying.

Erin voted for Barack Obama in 2008 and again in 2012. She started questioning the wisdom of doing the same thing in 2016. Her life and her family's lives had not gotten better, trade deals and automation had eroded the steel industry, and her hometown was suffering. Her parents and one brother were still in Weirton; another brother was in suburban Pittsburgh, and two others were out of state. For them, leaving the Democratic Party was like leaving the Catholic Church; they were devoted to both. They were ready for change; they just thought it would come from a Democrat. However, something clicked in all of them when Donald Trump came down the escalator at Trump Tower and talked about the dignity of work.

It was, as Erin explained, an awakening. The Brown and Koper families were families of hard work. They had punched their way up in this country, with a brother serving in the military, another working as a police officer, and the rest serving their communities in their own ways.

They were among and surrounded by middle-class people who worked with their hands as welders, barbers, small business owners, waitresses, and carpenters; they volunteered in their community and at their church, they coached neighborhood rec leagues and invested in making their neighborhoods safer and more beautiful.

These were the people who were about to be the center of the nation; people who lived in places like Weirton, nearby East Palestine, Ohio, and Butler, Pennsylvania. They all had a deep sense of place, of belonging to the land and to each other—they were part of something bigger than self. And one by one, they all began to question only one part of their identity: being part of the Democratic Party. It was a tectonic shift that spread slowly across the region, and unless you were asking about it, you would never have known it was happening. The people looked the same. The Brown family still did. So did the Koper family. They still held the same values. The people had not changed, but the Republican and Democratic Parties had changed, especially the Democratic Party, which lobbed off people like the Browns and the Kopers in favor of being the party of the ascendant.

And the Republicans were more than willing to take them in. Especially Trump.

At that time, Erin said she had voted straight ticket all of her life and nothing was getting better financially, personally, or in her community. It felt strangling, she said. So, along with her family, she started watching the Republican debates. Each time one was held, she felt more drawn to what Trump was saying he would do.

For Erin and her family, it was America first. Her parents, who came to the United States for a better life, instilled the importance of service and patriotism in their family. This spoke to Erin, and Trump said "America first" a lot.

The more the press attacked Trump, the more Erin felt that she needed to find balance to the news she was receiving. She was dumbfounded that the news organizations she had always trusted to tell the truth were now making her question their reliability. She started doing her own survey of the news. As a journalism major, she found this both easy and disheartening. How, she wondered, could the media be so biased? How had she never seen this before? Erin candidly admits to being very confused by the contrast between what she had believed for so long to be the tenets of good journalism and the goals of effective government. How could this be? Her father, mother, then-fiancé Jacob, and siblings all found themselves wondering the same thing.

Erin and Jacob's wedding took place just before the 2016 election. Weeks before the wedding, she felt isolated when most of her bridesmaids, during casual conversations over wine, talked about the upcoming election and were shocked to hear that she was considering going to the other side.

Erin was shocked that her views were considered controversial. She was even more shocked that those views would ultimately end friendships.

Trump spoke to her as a then-thirty-five-year-old adult who was getting married, in the process of buying a home, and paying for her wedding. When Election Day came around, most of Erin's family, including her parents, had changed their party registration to Republican. All of them voted for Trump.

But Erin waited to change her registration. Then came the Supreme Court justice hearings in 2018. Erin was watching the confirmation hearings for Brett Kavanaugh when something snapped. That something was then-Senator Kamala Harris and her contentious and controversial grilling of the future justice over sexual abuse allegations that had not a thread of evidence.

Erin changed her party registration that day; she was now a Republican.

Six months later, in January 2019, Erin's world was rocked when her father John passed away at eighty-four. His death created a hole in her life and left her looking for purpose. She was supposed to be doing something. What was it? She found that purpose one year later when COVID-19 hit. She noticed that few people were applying common sense to the pandemic, so she decided to do something her father had done in Democratic politics his entire life, including one last run for office at eighty, and that was to get involved in local politics.

Only this Brown would be getting involved in Republican politics. She said she felt as though her father was there, encouraging her. She signed up to do a Get Out the Vote class in Pittsburgh with Scott Presler, an outside-the-box, gay, conservative activist with long, flowing hair and an over-the-top persona, to learn how to sign up people to vote.

She failed. Miserably. She went out into the community with several other novices and was unable to sign up one person.

She wanted to give up. Her sense of her father's encouragement did not allow it. Neither did Presler. So she pressed on. Two weeks later, she went to another class Presler was giving in Butler. And everything clicked. Big time. Erin explains that she found her purpose. Within days, she was putting up her own voter registration tables wherever she could and registering voters. And she was good at it.

By the end of that presidential cycle, which Trump lost, Erin was fully engaged with the conservative populist movement to the point that she became the president of the Allegheny County Council of Republican Women, a volunteer organization designed to engage women in the political process.

People who were once her friends called her a Trumper. She would laugh. It was never about him; he was the result of the movement. Erin carried on.

She and Jacob were now Pittsburgh homeowners. Their hundred-year-old house is in the working-class Elliot section and has a breathtaking view of a city she now calls home, a city that has gone from being the jewel of Appalachia to one riddled with unchecked crime and hundreds of homeless camps littering the main thoroughfares. It is also the entry point for world travelers to the Great Allegheny Passage bike trail and the site of a vibrant open-air drug trade that has driven businesses and consumers away from the downtown and caused city residents to flee to rural counties.

Ed Gainey, a Democrat and Pittsburgh's first Black mayor, roared into office, unseating another Democrat, as a social justice warrior who danced around the "defund police" mantra and called for reforming the police as one of his key campaign tenets.

As crime rose, the Pittsburgh Bureau of Police under Gainey did not submit its annual crime numbers to the FBI, making it difficult for police and citizens to get a true picture of crime in the city—but not residents like Erin and Jacob. People who lived and worked in the city knew differently. They saw the crime happening in front of them; they saw it with their own eyes, heard it on the police scanner or on the nightly news; this was their home, and it was being run to the ground, just as Weirton was—all under Democrats.[1]

Gainey also failed to fully staff the police force, which had gone from over one thousand officers to under 850.[2] Gainey bragged that crime was down. It wasn't. Then the Gainey administration decided to eliminate a desk officer from all of the Pittsburgh police stations from 3:00 to 7:00 a.m.[3]

People left. So did businesses. Pittsburgh's office market went into a recession, plagued by increasing vacancy rates, low rent growth, and very little new construction.[4]

But the Steel City was not alone in its struggles. The same thing was happening in the county and the country.

While Gainey, along with Rep. Summer Lee and Allegheny County chief executive Sara Innamorato (all Democrats, with the latter two getting their start in the Democratic Socialists of America Pittsburgh chapter), spent their time railing about losing abortion access[5]—something that was never going to happen in Pennsylvania—the city was collapsing as business after business began retreating[6] from the crime and drug dealing and relocating outside of the city.

Like many Americans living in cities across the country they loved, the crime wave hit Erin hard. It was personal. She was bewildered by how the Democratic Party she had identified with for so long ignored violent crime in the name of social justice.

Erin's world had been rocked weeks earlier in June 2024. An eighteen-year-old college freshman, Sofia Mancing, from, yes, Butler, was interning at Flying Scooter Productions in downtown Pittsburgh after finishing her sophomore year at the University of Southern California in Los Angeles. After only one week on the job, Mancing was viciously attacked by a homeless woman in broad daylight. The woman came from out of nowhere and smacked her hard in the back of the head with a shoe.

Shaken, Mancing said she kept walking briskly, hoping the woman would move along.

She did not. The woman followed her down the sidewalk, grabbed her by the hair, pulled her into the street, and shoved her onto the ground. She then started punching and kicking her in the face, in the back of the head, and along her shoulders and back.

Then she dragged her farther into the street and into oncoming traffic.

Mancing was eventually rushed to the hospital with a concussion and a broken nose. She was lucky to be alive.

What made the entire attack even more horrific was that people stood around watching and did nothing while Mancing desperately tried to defend herself. The entire attack, and the lack of assistance, was captured on a city camera.

The Pittsburgh Bureau of Police said the video showed that the attacker intended to cause severe injury to Mancing; police found the woman, Shurontaya Festa, and arrested and charged her with aggravated assault and disorderly conduct.

The co-owners of Flying Scooter Productions sent a statement to local news organizations saying their company had opened its doors in downtown Pittsburgh seven years ago, and they've seen a steady increase in crime, drug dealing, and homelessness in that area.

The statement also said, "We have had enough of the egregious oversight and performative rhetoric. We are asking the elected officials to do what is needed to make Pittsburgh safe—because regardless of what they are telling you—it is far from it."

The day after the attack, Erin was at home seething over what happened on a main street she could see from her home overlooking the city. She was furious that not one elected official stepped up and made a statement. She was also scared. That could have been her. That could have been her sister, her mother. It felt personal. She felt helpless as she sat curled up on her couch in her living room.

The phone rang. She didn't get up. It went to voicemail. She didn't listen. Then the *ping* went off, indicating that she was getting a text.

The call she had missed was from the Trump campaign in Florida. They wanted to talk to her about something. The president wanted the focus at the convention to be on everyday people from across the country, people he said had skin in the game. To Erin's great shock, they asked her if she had any interest in speaking at the convention on prime-time television. The focus that night was on the impact crime was having on everyday Americans.

She told them, *Have I got a story to tell you.*

Two weeks later, she and Jacob were on a plane to Wisconsin. They left on Sunday, July 14, the day after the assassination attempt on Trump in Butler.

———

Erin hears the announcer say, "Erin Koper of Pittsburgh, Pennsylvania." She is now calm. She is going to do exactly what Huckabee told her and give them hell.

Game on, she tells herself, and walks out.

Good evening. My name is Erin Koper. I'm a grassroots organizer, a proud Republican woman, and a longtime resident of Pittsburgh, Pennsylvania. I'm here to urge Americans to reelect President Trump and make America safe again.

But I'm also here with a warning because in recent years, I've had a front row seat to the chaos caused by Democrats and their soft-on-crime policies. Democrat mayor Ed Gainey, congresswoman Summer Lee, and especially Socialist county executive Sara Innamorato have demoralized and disrespected our police while unleashing criminals into our communities.

The Pittsburgh Police Department has shrunk from 991 officers in 2020 to 750 at the end of last year. Response times are soaring. One city worker got mugged at gunpoint and raced to a police station, but no one was there to help. The Democrats have given Pittsburgh defund the police on steroids. The result is crime and chaos.

There were 122 murders in my county in 2022, one of the deadliest years on record. Drug deaths are also near record highs.

But statistics don't tell the full story.

I've been chased by drug dealers on my own streets. I've seen filthy tent cities pop up on my block. I've talked to business owners who find human waste, used needles, and shell casings outside their shops.

I felt the chill of fear as a woman when I'm alone in a parking garage or on the street. What the Democrats did to San Francisco, they're doing to my city.

But law-abiding citizens are fighting back and saying, no more. I saw this when Pittsburgh Republicans, independents, even Democrats came together to beat Soros prosecutor last November.

It can happen again this November.

If we stand together, we will beat the soft-on-crime Democrats and make our streets safe again. We can reelect President Trump, and we can save our cities. Thank you.

Erin walked off the stage. She had stopped shaking before she went on. She and Jacob stayed one more day. They were home watching President Trump when he took the stage Thursday night:

Friends, delegates, and fellow citizens. I stand before you this evening with a message of confidence, strength, and hope. Four months from now, we will have an incredible victory, and we will begin the four greatest years in the history of our country.

Together, we will launch a new era of safety, prosperity, and freedom for citizens of every race, religion, color, and creed.

The discord and division in our society must be healed. We must heal it quickly. As Americans, we are bound together by a single fate and a shared destiny. We rise together. Or we fall apart.

I am running to be president for all of America, not half of America, because there is no victory in winning for half of America.

So tonight, with faith and devotion, I proudly accept your nomination for president of the United States. Thank you. Thank you very much.

Thank you very much. And we will do it right. We're going to do it right.

Let me begin this evening by expressing my gratitude to the American people for your outpouring of love and support following the assassination attempt at my rally on Saturday.

As you already know, the assassin's bullet came within a quarter of an inch of taking my life. So many people have asked me what happened. "Tell us what happened, please." And therefore, I will tell you exactly what happened, and you'll never hear it from me a second time, because it's actually too painful to tell.

It was a warm, beautiful day in the early evening in Butler Township in the great Commonwealth of Pennsylvania. Music was loudly playing, and the campaign was doing really well. I went to the stage and the crowd was cheering wildly. Everybody was happy. I began speaking very strongly, powerfully, and happily. Because I was discussing the great job my administration did on immigration at the southern border. We were very proud of it.

Behind me, and to the right, was a large screen that was displaying a chart of border crossings under my leadership. The numbers were absolutely amazing. In order to see the chart, I started to, like this, turn to my right, and was ready to begin a little bit further turn, which I'm very lucky I didn't do, when I heard a loud whizzing sound and felt something hit me really, really hard. On my right ear. I said to myself, "Wow, what was that? It can only be a bullet."

And moved my right hand to my ear, brought it down. My hand was covered with blood. Just absolutely blood all over the place. I immediately knew it was very serious. That we were under attack. And in one movement proceeded to drop to the ground. Bullets were continuing to fly as very brave Secret Service agents rushed to the stage. And they really did. They rushed to the stage.

These are great people at great risk, I will tell you, and [they] pounced on top of me so that I would be protected. There was blood pouring everywhere, and yet in a certain way I felt very safe because I had God on my side. I felt that.

The amazing thing is that prior to the shot, if I had not moved my head at that very last instant, the assassin's bullet would have perfectly hit its mark and I would not be here tonight. We would not be together. The most incredible aspect of what took place on that terrible evening, in the fading sun, was actually seen later. In almost all cases, as you probably know. And when even a single bullet is fired, just a single bullet, and we had many bullets that were being fired, crowds run for the exits or stampede. But not in this case. It was very unusual.

This massive crowd of tens of thousands of people stood by and didn't move an inch. In fact, many of them bravely but automatically stood up, looking for where the sniper would be. They knew immediately that it was a sniper. And then began pointing at him. You can see that if you look at the group behind me. That was just a small group compared to what was in front.

Nobody ran and, by not stampeding, many lives were saved. But that isn't the reason that they didn't move. The reason is that they knew I was in very serious trouble. They saw it. They saw me go down. They saw the blood, and thought, actually most did, that I was dead.

They knew it was a shot to the head. They saw the blood. And there's an interesting statistic. The ears are the bloodiest part. If something happens with the ears they bleed more than any other part of the body. For whatever reason the doctors told me that.

And I said, "Why is there so much blood?"

He said, "It's the ears, they bleed more."

So we learned something. But they just—

They just, this beautiful crowd, they didn't want to leave me. They knew I was in trouble. They didn't want to leave me. And you can see that love written all over their faces. True.

Incredible people. They're incredible people. Bullets were flying over us, yet I felt serene. But now the Secret Service agents were putting themselves in peril. They were in very dangerous territory.

Bullets were flying right over them, missing them by a very small amount of inches. And then it all stopped. Our Secret Service sniper, from a much greater distance and with only one bullet used, took the assassin's life. Took him out.

I'm not supposed to be here tonight. Not supposed to be here.

When he says that, the hall bursts into chants of "Yes, you are."

Thank you. But I'm not. And I'll tell you. I stand before you in this arena only by the grace of almighty God.

And watching the reports over the last few days, many people say it was a providential moment. Probably was. When I rose, surrounded by Secret Service, the crowd was confused because they thought I was dead. And there was great, great sorrow. I could see that on their faces as I looked out. They didn't know I was looking out; they thought it was over.

But I could see it and I wanted to do something to let them know I was OK. I raised my right arm, looked at the thousands and thousands of people that were breathlessly waiting and started shouting, "Fight, fight, fight."

Once my clenched fist went up, and it was high into the air, you've all seen that, the crowd realized I was OK and roared with pride for our country like no crowd I have ever heard before. Never heard anything like it.

For the rest of my life, I will be grateful for the love shown by that giant audience of patriots that stood bravely on that fateful evening in Pennsylvania. Tragically, the shooter claimed the life of one of our fellow Americans: Corey Comperatore. Unbelievable person, everybody tells me. Unbelievable.

And seriously wounded two other great warriors. Spoke to them today: David Dutch and James Copenhaver. Two great people. I also spoke to all three families of these tremendous people.

Our love and prayers are with them and always will be. We're never going to forget them. They came for a great rally. They were serious Trumpsters, I want to tell you. They were serious Trumpsters and still are. But Corey, unfortunately, we have to use the past tense.

He was incredible. Yeah. He was a highly respected former fire chief. Respected by everybody. Was accompanied by his wife, Helen. Incredible woman. I spoke to her today. Devastated. And two precious daughters. He lost his life selflessly acting as a human shield to protect them from flying bullets. He went right over the top of them and was hit. What a fine man he was.

Trump stops speaking. He looks behind him. On the stage with him is Corey's fire helmet and jacket, which his family had shipped that day to Milwaukee and which had been placed on the stage just as Trump began his speech.

He points to the jacket and helmet. The crowd is chanting, "Corey, Corey, Corey."

Trump walks over to the helmet and jacket of the fifty-year-old Sarver, Pennsylvania, father, husband, and volunteer firefighter who had died five days earlier while shielding his family from gunfire when Thomas Crooks opened fire on Trump during the Butler rally.

He embraces the shoulders of the jacket. He kisses the helmet. He says, "Thank you." He looks at the crowd, points to the jacket, and mouths, "Thank him."

"Corey, Corey, Corey!" The crowd is on its feet chanting.

"I want to thank the fire department and the family for sending his helmet, his outfit and it was just something, and they're going to do something very special when they get it."

Trump then asks the crowd to observe a moment of silence in honor of Corey.

There is no greater love than to lay down one's life for others. This is the spirit that forged America in her darkest hours. And this is the love that will lead America back to the summit of human achievement and greatness. This is what we need.

Despite such a heinous attack, we unite this evening, more determined than ever. I am more determined than ever and so are you. So is everybody in this room.

Thank you. Thank you very much. Our resolve is unbroken and our purpose is unchanged, to deliver a government that serves the American people better than ever before. Nothing will stop me in this mission, because our vision is righteous and our cause is pure.

No matter what obstacle comes our way, we will not break. We will not bend. We will not back down and I will never stop fighting for you, your family and our magnificent country. Never.

And everything I have to give with all of the energy and fight in my heart and soul, I pledge to our nation tonight. Thank you very much. I pledge that to our nation. We're going to turn our nation around and we're going to do it very quickly. Thank you.

This election should be about the issues facing our country and how to make America successful, safe, free and great again.

In an age when our politics too often divide us, now is the time to remember that we are all fellow citizens—we are one nation under God, indivisible, with liberty and justice for all.

For the first twenty-eight minutes, Trump held the room spellbound. When he was halfway through his speech, for thirty-eight minutes, he went through the business of what it was like being president and what it was like not being president. He then returned to meet the moment.

So, to conclude, just a few short days ago, my journey with you nearly ended. We know that. And yet, here we are tonight, all gathered together, talking about the future, promise and a total renewal of a thing we love very much.

It's called America.

We live in a world of miracles. None of us knows God's plan, or where life's adventure will take us.

But if the events of last Saturday make anything clear, it is that every single moment we have on Earth is a gift from God. We have to make the most of every day for the people and for the country that we love.

The attacker in Pennsylvania wanted to stop our movement, but the truth is, the movement has never been about me. It has always been about you. It's your movement. It's the biggest movement in the history of our country by far. It can't be stopped. It can't be stopped. It has always been about the hardworking, patriotic citizens of America.

For too long, our nation has settled for too little. We settled for too little. We've given everything to other nations, to other people. You have been told to lower your expectations and to accept less for your families.

I am here tonight with the opposite message: Your expectations are not big enough. They're not big enough. It is time to start expecting and demanding the best leadership in the world, leadership that is bold, dynamic, relentless and fearless. We can do that.

We are Americans. Ambition is our heritage. Greatness is our birthright.

But as long as our energies are spent fighting each other, our destiny will remain out of reach. And that's not acceptable. We must instead take that energy and use it to realize our country's true potential—and write our own thrilling chapter of the American story. We can do it together. We will unite. We are going to come together and success will bring us together.

It is a story of love, sacrifice and so many other things. And remember the word: Devotion. It's unmatched devotion. Our American ancestors crossed the Delaware, survived the icy winter at Valley Forge and defeated a mighty empire to establish our cherished republic.

They fought so hard, they lost so many. They pushed thousands and thousands of miles across a dangerous frontier, taming the wilderness to build a life and a magnificent home for their family. They packed their families into covered wagons, trekked across hazardous trails. Scaled towering mountains and braved rivers and rapids to stake their claim on the wide-open, new and very beautiful frontier. When our way of life was threatened, American patriots marched onto the battlefield, raced into enemy strongholds and stared down death—and stared down those enemies—to keep alive the flame of freedom. At Yorktown, Gettysburg, and Midway, they joined the roll call of immortal heroes. So many—just so many heroes, so many great, great people. And we have to cherish those people. We can't forget those people. We have to cherish those people.

And building monuments to those great people is a good thing, not a bad thing. They saved our country. No challenge was too much. No hardship was too great. No enemy was too fierce. Together, these patriots soldiered on and endured, and they prevailed. Because they had faith in each other, faith in their country, and above all, they had faith in their God.

Just like our ancestors, we must now come together, rise above past differences. Any disagreements have to be put aside, and go forward united as one people, one nation, pledging allegiance to one great, beautiful—I think it's so beautiful—American flag.

Tonight, I ask for your partnership, for your support and I am humbly asking for your vote. I want your vote. We're going to make our country great again. Every day, I will strive to honor the trust you have placed in me, and I will never, ever let you down. I promise that. I will never let you down.

To all of the forgotten men and women who have been neglected, abandoned and left behind, you will be forgotten no longer. We will press forward, and together, we will win, win, win.

Nothing will sway us. Nothing will slow us. And no one will ever stop us.

No matter what dangers come our way, no matter what obstacles lie in our path, we will keep striving toward our shared and glorious destiny—and we will not fail. We will not fail.

Together, we will save this country, we will restore the republic, and we will usher in the rich and wonderful tomorrows that our people so truly deserve.

America's future will be bigger, better, bolder, brighter, happier, stronger, freer, greater and more united than ever before.

And quite simply put, we will very quickly make America great again.

Thank you very much. Thank you very much, Wisconsin. God bless you, God bless you, Wisconsin, and God bless the United States of America, our great country. Thank you very much, everybody. Thank you.

For Erin, Trump's emotion-driven, sometimes rambling acceptance of his party's nomination just days after an assassin tried to kill him was everything she hoped it would be. The people she saw at the convention weren't just luminaries like DeSantis and Haley, two people she thought effectively gave the vibe that the party was unified despite past differences. Rather, it was the people like her who were given the opportunity to show that the everyman was there and part of this party that made her feel confident about the election.

What riveted her that Thursday was Trump's naked emotion in telling his perspective of how a bullet "came within a quarter of an inch of taking my life."

When Trump said that a second relating of the event would be "too painful to tell," it was something he and I would discuss over and over again as waves of emotions would hit him in those conversations. Those interviews, more like conversations, would all start in less than ten days at a series of rallies in Pennsylvania.

For Erin, it was a convention for the people, and she believed it showcased a coalition that included former Democrats like herself, college-educated women, and middle-class neighbors of all races with whom she lived and worked. Erin believed there was a change afoot. She also believed that few saw it, even though she felt it was right in front of the world if they had watched that convention and heard her story as well as scores of other average Americans who told their stories that week.

It made sense to her to see rapper Amber Rose, wrestler Hulk Hogan, and evangelical leader Franklin Graham there. The appearance of these personalities jolted the press, Democrats, and even some Republicans.

Outside the arena that day, delegates were playing cornhole, some wore bandages on their ear in support of Trump and his injury. Democrats and the press, however, were focused on the frenzied push to force President Joe Biden off the ticket and replace him with Vice President Kamala Harris, the favorite among the ruling class. Biden being forced out was seemingly gaining traction. The story of the attempted assassination of a president seemed less important to the ruling class than a sitting president getting forced out of running one hundred days before an election. The fact that Biden was defiant about staying made the story even more salacious.

Chris LaCivita told me that night that if Harris did replace Biden, the first thing the Trump campaign would call her would be Biden's "border czar."

The same night that Trump was to take the stage, the *New York Times* asked Florida Senator Marco Rubio if he was nervous about the possibility of Kamala Harris taking over from Joe Biden. Rubio smiled. "Is that like a real question? Or is that a—listen, I don't have anything against her, but she's like a real, full-blown left-winger."

Three days later, everything would change. Again.

Chapter 6

"Now the Fun Begins..."

MILWAUKEE, Wisconsin
July 18, 2024

Chris LaCivita was pacing, scrolling through X (formerly Twitter). Donald Trump had just finished delivering his convention speech. It was ninety minutes long, and LaCivita expected the usual hair-on-fire reaction from the national press.

It was there, all right. Kyle Cheney from *Politico* posted, "Trump has officially entered the second day of his speech."[1] *Not too bad*, LaCivita thought. It was interesting to watch the reporters step up their sharing of veteran journalist Mark Halperin's report from earlier that day, citing sources close to President Joe Biden who said Biden would soon drop out of the race, likely by the end of the weekend.

It was clear to LaCivita that the reaction to Trump's speech and the success of the Republican National Convention (RNC) had put Democrats and the news media on edge. LaCivita, Trump's campaign manager Susie Wiles, and Trump had all done the impossible: unified the party at the convention, showcased regular people who reflected the voters they wanted to reach across the country, and seemingly had a pretty good time doing it.

While the festivities took place all week in Milwaukee, elected Democrats began urging Biden to drop out. Senator Martin Heinrich of New Mexico called for him to step aside, and Wisconsin representative Mark Pocan, who just days earlier had joined Biden in Madison, said, "It's time to pass the torch."[2] Hollywood A-lister George Clooney was out, which meant the big money was out. Michael Moritz, Silicon Valley investor and megadonor, posted the cryptic message: "The clock has run out."[3]

LaCivita chuckled to himself. History-making events were happening right now. Halperin was a solid journalist who didn't just put things out there to see if they would stick. If he was reporting that Biden might drop out, he probably would.

Less than five days earlier, LaCivita was in his Milwaukee hotel room-turned-office, again pacing, with iPhone in hand, looking at texts. He made an oblong pattern from wall to wall while he checked with RNC staff about lighting for the convention floor stage and kept an eye on the oversized flat-screen on the wall.

It was Saturday, July 13, 2024, and he was waiting for President Trump's arrival onstage in Butler, Pennsylvania, a city less than forty miles from where LaCivita was born.

The door to LaCivita's room was slightly ajar—a practice he follows so that RNC staffers and his daughter Victoria, who was working on the campaign, could easily enter.

LaCivita had been in Milwaukee for a week as chief operating officer for the RNC. LaCivita also shared cocampaign chair duties with Susie Wiles.

Out of the corner of his eye, LaCivita saw Trump walk onto the stage in Butler, but then he was momentarily distracted by a staffer's text about a minor staging snafu. Suddenly, there was running down the hall and his daughter burst through his door.

"Dad, they shot the president!" she said.

LaCivita whipped around to look at the TV; he'd only turned away for a moment. He saw Trump, surrounded by Secret Service agents, pumping his fist in the air, saying, "Fight, fight, fight!"

A US Marine veteran who had served in the Persian Gulf War, LaCivita has a reputation for being stoic in emergencies, despite his larger-than-life personality the rest of the time. He quickly assessed the situation: yes, there was blood trickling down the side of Trump's face, but he was standing, so that was a good sign. LaCivita watched Nick, the agent who had grabbed the former president by the collar, and he seemed calm—another good sign. When Trump seemed to resist the agents who were trying to carry him off the stage, LaCivita took a deep breath and let it out slowly.

That's the guy I know. He wants to walk off by himself, so perhaps nothing vital was hit.

LaCivita quickly dialed Susie Wiles. The two are close, a rarity in American politics, especially when both people share power. *What the hell?* he asked, then said that from his vantage point, Trump seemed to be okay despite the bleeding. Wiles was getting into the car with Trump and promised to call back.

Two hours later, she did. She was incredulous, but not for the reason one might think. Trump was handling the situation by cracking jokes and telling stories with the hospital staff, she said.

LaCivita smiled to himself. *There is no way God would spare Trump only for him to lose the election*, he thought. Especially in Pennsylvania, of all places, a state that represents everything that is part of this conservative populist movement. Now he knew that Trump would win.

LaCivita spent the rest of the evening fielding calls and text messages from the press. His calls with reporters were unpleasant, mostly because he yelled at the ones who were impatient to post something online or broadcast the news. Almost no one wanted to wait for details. It was infuriating. The first headline LaCivita saw was on CNN, fifty minutes after Trump was shot: "Trump injured in incident at Pennsylvania rally."[4]

LaCivita lost it. *What the hell is an "incident"? Damn them; he was shot at—shot!*

Irate, he called a CNN senior exec to raise hell, asking that they change the headline. The same thing happened with the *Washington Post*, which insinuated that it wasn't a bullet that struck Trump but pieces of glass that clipped his ear, a story that would linger for weeks.[5] LaCivita wanted to know: How the fuck did *they* know what hit him? Did they have a ballistics report? Did they have information no one else did?

Born in McKeesport, Pennsylvania, the son of a first-generation Italian father and a first-generation Irish mother, LaCivita has lived a life that embodies the rich traditions and cultural connections found in many western Pennsylvania manufacturing communities. He also personifies the take-no-prisoners rough edges that come from such a background.

He's one of five brothers from a devoutly Catholic, close-knit family. The LaCivita crew left the region in 1978 when his father took a job in Richmond at Reynolds Aluminum just as the steel and manufacturing industry collapsed—a collapse that would lead to other industries folding.

It was a fracturing of place that happened across the Rust Belt, and it went on for decades. The overall impact is still being felt—many churches closed, along with the schools attached to them. Barbershops, social clubs, and houses were boarded up because no one could sell them.

Drive through these cities, and the ghosts of the boarded-up buildings still stand—many reduced to shells of what had once been as if anyone who stuck around needed to be reminded.

Mighty McKeesport, once the fastest-growing municipality in the nation and such a politically important locality that candidate John F. Kennedy campaigned there in 1960, had fallen apart by 1980, just a few years after the LaCivita family left for Virginia.

Walk the empty streets of McKeesport today, and you'll see scar tissue from wounds that have never healed.

LaCivita acknowledges being an average student in school, more interested in mischief than getting high grades. He found college less than inspiring until a political science professor spurred him into a challenge over the merits of government-funded health care. In 1990, his Marine Corps artillery reserve unit was activated, and, in 1991, he found himself in the middle of the Persian Gulf War. Five months later, he returned home with a Purple Heart, scars on his face, and two cracked ribs from shrapnel.

That tough marine psyche and western Pennsylvania work ethic remain very much a part of who LaCivita is, so he spent most of July 13 and 14 creating new friends in the news media. His boss, the former president of the United States, had just survived an assassination attempt in the most dramatic fashion possible, and yet the media were still trying to find ways to poke him.

By Saturday evening on July 13, as Trump was about to be discharged from the hospital, the team debated whether he should return to Bedminster, New Jersey, or head straight to Wisconsin for the convention.

Wiles called LaCivita later that night to say they would go to Bedminster.

———

July 18, 2024

As the convention drew to a close and people poured out of the hall, LaCivita and Wiles took a few moments to reflect on the event's successes. They stood on the convention floor, with balloons bouncing around them, and agreed it had met the moment.

From the beginning, LaCivita, Wiles, pollster Tony Fabrizio, and deputy campaign manager Justin Caporale had decided that instead of holding a convention driven by politicians' speeches, they would allow some politicians to speak but not let them be the main driver of Trump's message. Instead, they wanted ordinary Americans to talk about their lives, their aspirations, or their concerns about safety, security, the economy—people whose stories could demonstrate what needed to change in the country.

It capped a campaign that contrasted what was, under Trump, and what is, under Biden. And who better to communicate that than regular Joes who had a story to tell, like the Gold Star families of fallen troops during Biden's catastrophic withdrawal from Afghanistan.

Videos created by LaCivita and John Brabender, another western Pennsylvania native, that introduced each speaker hit just the right notes—it was fascinating to watch the impact the speakers had on people throughout the state, who perhaps saw themselves or their communities through the speakers' experiences, and to contrast their reactions with those of the national press who, for the most part, failed to realize the impact.

LaCivita was amazed: the organizers executed their job flawlessly, and the convention drove home a powerful message with the theme that everyone is welcome to be part of the conservative populist coalition, and that people no longer would feel forgotten in a Trump second term.

Just days before Trump had been shot, the RNC had completed something that had never been done before—it trashed the party platform, rewrote it, condensed it in the vision of Donald Trump, and produced a to-the-point document that would redefine the Republican Party going forward.

LaCivita was satisfied with the result. The new document wasn't filled with swamp-lobbyist-written bullshit.

He was also not overly concerned about whether Halperin's report on Biden quitting the race was true. "I'm not afraid if it's [Kamala] Harris," he told me that day. "If it's Harris, she's the border czar." And that was that.

The possibility that Harris would become the Democrats' nominee had been discussed by the Trump team since before the fateful June 27 debate between Trump and Biden. The team had written an eleven-page memo in May titled "Nominating an Alternative Democratic Presidential Candidate" and distributed it among top Trump campaign aides.

The scenarios outlined included Biden stepping aside, an insider rebellion, and an act of God. In the days following the debate, as pressure mounted from the national press—which had until then been sympathetic to Biden or ignored his cognitive decline—the Trump campaign began preparing for what seemed to be inevitable.

LaCivita and Wiles had become convinced that Biden was on his way out. By July 19, the question was whether he'd drop out or be forced out. LaCivita, Wiles, and other team members discussed various perspectives. They knew that every video and every message they put forth during the convention was based on the knowledge that there was a better than 50 percent chance of Harris becoming the nominee.

So the message being pushed was that this was the Biden-Harris administration. The videos shown during the convention cast the opponent as Biden-Harris, and LaCivita knew that some of Trump's detractors in the press would report that the Trump campaign wasn't ready for Kamala Harris. And if they did, it would prove to LaCivita that they had not been paying attention to the Republicans' messaging.

————

It was now Sunday, July 21, 2024, three days after the RNC convention had ended and eight days since Trump was shot. The squeeze on Biden from longtime friends, campaign donors, and congressional leaders had taken a toll on the eighty-one-year-old president, who was recovering from COVID-19 at his home in Delaware. His poll numbers were abysmal, and a series of national interviews and public speeches meant to reassure the public that he was in command of his abilities since the debate had the opposite effect.

Outwardly, Biden appeared dug in. The calls and visits kept coming. Confidants told the president that if he stayed in the race, Trump would win in a landslide. Biden attempted to argue otherwise, insisting that he was the only one who could defeat Trump.

He convinced no one.

Then, at 1:46 p.m. (EST), Biden posted on X: "While it has been my intention to seek reelection, I believe it is in the best interest of my party and the country for me to stand down and to focus solely on fulfilling my duties as president for my term."[6] He promised to address the nation that week.

Within short order—twenty-eight minutes, to be exact—Biden endorsed Vice President Kamala Harris as the Democratic Party's nominee.

LaCivita was in a Fort Lauderdale hotel room, on the phone with Tony and Susie, when it happened. They concluded that the campaign was going to get fun. Why? Because they all knew what would happen: Harris would have a honeymoon moment, and then she would collapse the Democratic Party vote.

LaCivita knew the Democrats could see what he was seeing—that Trump would easily beat Biden. They also saw the trajectory of the campaign post-convention, so they made the unprecedented move of deposing the incumbent president and swapping in the vice president—a vice president who, until recently, had not been well regarded and was even considered a joke in some political circles.

Within minutes of Biden's endorsement, LaCivita's and Wiles's instincts were proven correct: Harris *was* canonized. She was now, to Democrats, without sin and without fault, and she didn't have to say or do anything for the news media. All she had to do was exist, and she would be ordained the next president.

And thus began the coronation period.

———

LaCivita, Fabrizio, and Wiles had video and audio clips of Harris talking about immigration, fracking, and transgender surgeries for prisoners paid for by taxpayers, and they were ready to push back. For over a year, Trump had dominated the news cycle, and they knew that was about to end and that every story about Harris in the mainstream media would be positive.

LaCivita also knew that stories casting the Trump campaign as "demoralized" were about to become the narrative.

But he knew that could not be further from the truth. He expected bedwetters in the Republican Party—a lot of whom who were not involved in the campaign but wanted to be—would line up to give anonymous quotes to an overly eager press excited to tell the story of a campaign now in shambles.

LaCivita gritted his teeth. *They don't know shit.*

Trump never once lost faith in his team. LaCivita and Wiles were professionals who had been through tougher campaigns; they knew the drill. They would focus on the mission and the plan and worry only about their execution.

LaCivita put out memo after memo to the press, explaining that Harris had consolidated the Democratic vote and that Trump's numbers had never gone down.

But the national press narrative became this: Harris had a bump, a two-percentage-point bounce. Yet, out in the field as a reporter, I struggled to find that bump among the voters who mattered in Pennsylvania, Michigan, and Wisconsin, where I headed for a week to figure out how the race might play out.

In Detroit, I found United Auto Workers union members holding an impromptu pro-Trump rally on a corner outside a Stellantis Mack assembly plant on Jean Avenue. Their national union president Shawn Fain had just endorsed Harris, and they planned to vote for Trump. It was a diverse working-class crowd, and they held American and Trump flags as union truck drivers dropped off or picked up loads from the plant.

No one in the local press covered it. No one in the national press covered it either. They did not see what was happening in the counties that mattered in Michigan. They were also missing the counties that mattered in Wisconsin and Pennsylvania. It wasn't the big cities; it was the working-class counties like Macomb, Erie, and Kenosha.

These three states are part of the famed "blue wall": Rust Belt states filled with working-class voters, just like the ones lined up on Jean Avenue, who nearly always vote the same way. Pennsylvania typically goes just a hair more to the left than Michigan and Wisconsin.

If Pennsylvania was suddenly leaning toward Harris, the other two states should be following suit. It wasn't happening. In fact, my reporting from Michigan and Wisconsin in the early days of Harris's campaign showed the opposite. I was once again straddling two worlds—one was on X, where national reporters at CNN, the *New York Times, Politico, Axios,* and the *Washington Post* were all reporting that Harris was transformational. Harris had a bump. Harris appealed to suburban women. Harris appealed to Black and Hispanic Americans.

My reporting showed a different experience. How could I be so off? But was I off? I didn't think so.

Nine days after Biden dropped out, Harris won enough virtual votes from Democratic delegates to secure her party's nomination for president. She officially became the first Black woman and first Asian American to lead a major-party ticket.

The party also had just unanimously nominated someone who had never earned a single vote from Democratic primary voters.

Just four years earlier, right after Thanksgiving Day in 2019, Harris had dropped out of the race for her party's nomination for president before the first vote was cast in Iowa. *Politico* wrote at the time that she ended her presidential campaign after months of failing to lift her candidacy from the bottom of the field; she was a candidate who was once touted by an adoring press as the "female Obama" and a marquee contender for the party's nomination.[7]

I covered her primary campaign that year. At first, she soared. Her announcement speech in her home state of California drew thousands of supporters as she portrayed herself as the best candidate to take on Trump. And her performance at a July 2019 debate received national attention after she ambushed former Vice President Joe Biden about his stance on school busing decades earlier.

Harris's peak didn't last long. By September 2019, she had dropped down to last place, and she could not pull herself up from the bottom of the heap.

After Biden won the primary contests in 2020, the one-time moderate Democrat who had always touted his working-class roots from Scranton, Pennsylvania, shocked the country when he picked Harris as his running mate. She was known to hold political views far to the left of his and was not considered to be politically astute.

Biden was among the few Democrats who could potentially win back the working class from Trump, and he eventually did so, barely, in 2020. He had considered four women for the vice presidency: Harris, Senator Elizabeth Warren of Massachusetts, Michigan governor Gretchen Whitmer, and Susan E. Rice, Obama's former national security adviser.

Despite reservations within the Biden camp and Harris's blistering attack on Biden in that July 2019 debate, Harris's ability to debate and the racial diversity she brought to the ticket elevated her above the other contenders, and she became Biden's running mate.

After the Biden-Harris ticket won, Harris performed bleakly as vice president. She waffled in her role of overseeing the migrant crisis at the southern border—in fact, she never went to the border in her nearly four years as vice president, as the issue escalated to become one of the biggest failures of the administration to voters in that cycle. For three years, her appearances on national television and at events were cringeworthy, even in the eyes of many in her party, and the culture in her office was toxic. By July 2024, the *Washington Post* reported, nearly 92 percent of the staff members she initially hired in 2021 had left.[8]

Now here she was, the Democratic nominee for president, less than a week after the press and her own party members had said she was not up to the role. Not only that; she was being heralded as the second coming of Barack Obama.

When I asked the chief of staff to a Pennsylvania congressman if he would have preferred her or Biden at the top of the ticket, he confessed, "For us, it would be better that it was Biden. I don't think my party understands that outside of DC and some cocktail parties in big cities, Harris has even less appeal in the state of Pennsylvania to voters than former Secretary of State Hillary Clinton."

He wasn't wrong. At least with Clinton, there was some semblance of connection; she was baptized in Scranton, Pennsylvania, and her family had roots there: Her father grew up in Scranton, and Clinton spent her summers at the family cabin in nearby Lake Winola, Wyoming County.

Biden, a son of Scranton, had picked off just enough working-class votes from Trump in 2020, thanks in large part to two things: COVID-19 and Biden's years-long association with rank-and-file union workers in the state. Biden spent an inordinate amount of time in Pennsylvania, not just to benefit himself when running with Obama in 2008 and 2012 but also during his own presidential bid. He would show up for local races for state House and state Senate, and voters believed he was one of them. Biden argued that he could hold onto those voters—but Harris? To anyone who knows the state and its voters, this would be a steep uphill climb.

Pennsylvania was a must-win for Democrats. Trump could win without it, so suggestions immediately began to surface that Pennsylvania governor Josh Shapiro, a moderate and popular Democrat who won his gubernatorial race two years earlier with a fair amount of support from Trump voters, should be Harris's vice-presidential pick.

Both Shapiro and Bob Casey, the Scranton Democrat who had been in the US Senate and held statewide office in some capacity since 1996, had steadfastly refused to acknowledge that Biden had problems before he dropped out. Casey would take the bigger hit because he was up for reelection.

When Harris stepped in, Shapiro and Casey released their full support for her; however, local Democrats were queasy. Harris did not support fracking, a main economic driver in the state. She hadn't pushed back on Biden's moratorium on liquid natural gas exports, which hurt the industry and farmers who depended on the royalties. She had been Biden's point person on the border, and the flood of fentanyl into Pennsylvania had claimed lives and taken its toll on small and large cities.

Senator John Fetterman, a centrist Democrat from the old steel town of Braddock, who won his seat the same year Shapiro did, was downright belligerent about Biden being pushed out. On the day Biden was pushed out, as members of the press and his fellow Democrats gushed their welcomes for Harris, Fetterman quipped, "Spare me the soaring accolades from people with their fingerprints on the blades in our president's back."[9]

Fetterman's reaction wasn't singular. Lifelong Democrat Shirley Hall in Blair County didn't just change her mind about whom she would vote for; she changed her party registration after Trump was shot and Biden was pushed out.

Sitting in her Tyrone home outside of Altoona the day Biden dropped out, Hall told me in an interview her decision happened for several reasons.[10] "The last three years under this administration have disheartened me, in how my party handled inflation, never recognizing that it is really impacting people's lives. Picking Harris shows me how out of touch they are with the working class. The party I always thought was for the little guy isn't anymore."

Nestled in the Appalachian foothills, Hall's modest home is like millions across the state and the Great Lakes Midwest. Hall embodies what few Democrats or the press apparently understand: a weariness about how detached the party had become from her, her community, and her sense of place.

Just down the road in Roaring Springs, the Appvion paper mill that had filled the valley with steam, jobs, and the sound of work echoing off the mountains had fallen victim to economic turbulence caused by the pandemic, government regulations, and multiple domestic and foreign owners far removed from the people and place where the plant had operated since 1866.

It was the last remaining manufacturing business there, and its downfall cost three hundred families their incomes; no one came to rescue the steelworkers who worked there. In the spring of 2024, the plant was leveled, and the valley was filled with the uneasy silence of loss.

"It was devastating," Hall said simply.

She pointed to Harris's indifference and dismissiveness regarding inflation and economic concerns in a state that, according to the most recent *ConsumerAffairs* report, had the largest increase in grocery prices year over year, making Pennsylvania families among the hardest hit in the country.[11]

As for Harris's vice-presidential pick, Shapiro seemed to be what she needed, at least on paper. He had an approval rating of over 60 percent among voters in the state, and when crises hit the state early in his administration—the toxic train derailment in East Palestine, Ohio, which happened on the state line and contaminated river communities downstream, and the collapse of an Interstate 95 ramp in Philadelphia—Shapiro handled his constituents' fear promptly and with executive leadership.

Shapiro's motto of "getting shit done" had cross-party appeal, and he made himself accessible to the press, unlike his predecessor, Governor Tom Wolf. He also gave a damn good speech.

The idea of Shapiro on the Harris ticket made some Republicans nervous—could he take her over the line? It made some Democrats nervous as well. Would he outshine Harris? Probably. Would her position on top issues such as fracking and border security and her views on "Medicare for all" be too far to his left for a partnership to work? Yes. Would his faith as a devout Jew make Shapiro a liability, given the antisemitism that was running deep in the party? No one said it out loud, outside of some on the far left, but it was there—and the Democrats needed the far left of their coalition intact to win.

Beyond Shapiro, Harris's choices had winnowed down to Senator Mark Kelly of Arizona and Minnesota governor Tim Walz.

As the search for Harris's vice president played out for all to see, LaCivita watched in amusement as the press committed their second-biggest gaslighting campaign: that Kamala Harris was the greatest thing since sliced bread. Their first gaslighting of the American people, of course, was that Joe Biden was fine, cognitively and physically, and had been fine for the past three years.

LaCivita and Wiles were patient. But soon, they were on TV defining Harris as dangerously liberal, beating her up rhetorically over her weak positions on crime, and then tying this weakness to the massive influx of migrants at the border. They continued to use her own voice, running ads to showcase her weaknesses on issues that matter to average Americans.

Trump's two advisers were consistently disciplined in pushing the message.

Conversely, the Harris campaign started running seven to fifteen different creatives in search of something that would stick with voters—they spent a lot of time trying to run ads that would define her to Americans. They could afford to do so since they were flush with money. All the donors in Hollywood, big business, and Democratic circles whose money had dried up since the Biden-Trump debate had opened up their pocketbooks again, and it was raining cash.

LaCivita watched as the press stalled attacking Trump—their focus was on Harris, and they were spinning their wheels. Meanwhile, MAGA Inc. was beating the living hell out of her. LaCivita and Wiles knew that Trump was fully defined in Americans' minds. Everyone knows who he is. LaCivita pulled out a variation of a line from comedian Danny Kaye and told the press right after Harris was crowned as the nominee that the Republican team's view of Kamala Harris was simple: "She is a blank canvas, and we hold a bucket of paint."[12]

He had used the same line during the February Republican primaries when telling the press how Trump had defeated former UN ambassador Nikki Haley.

On July 23, Tim Walz went on MSNBC's *Morning Joe* where he spent most of a four-minute interview discussing how divisional Republicans were, contrasting that with how excited the Democrats were about Harris as the nominee.

It was clear to LaCivita and Wiles that this was an audition.

"There's huge excitement. If it's any indication, my seventeen- and twenty-three-year-old kids said, 'TikTok's on fire.' They're back engaged. You can feel it. The donors are back," Walz said.

He was asked how important it would be for Harris to win the Midwest and about Trump's decision to pick Senator J. D. Vance of Ohio as his running mate. The Midwest is key, Walz said, and then launched into Vance with a vengeance.

"What I know is that people like J. D. Vance know nothing about small-town America. My town had four hundred people in it, twenty-four kids in my graduating class, twelve were cousins, and he gets it all wrong. It's not about hate, it's not about collapsing in. The golden rule there is 'mind your own damn business.' Their policies are what destroyed rural America. They've divided us. They're in our exam rooms. They're telling us what books to read. And I think what Kamala Harris knows is, bringing people together around the shared values, strong public schools, strong labor unions that create the middle class, health care that's affordable and accessible—those are the things."

LaCivita listened as Walz continued to label Trump and Vance as "divisional" and then landed the word he had obviously just been waiting to use.

"I think this is going back to the bread and butter, getting away from this division. We do not like what has happened, where we can't even go to Thanksgiving dinner with our uncle because you end up in some weird fight that is unnecessary. I think bringing back people together. . . . Well, it's true. These guys are just *weird*."

On a roll, Walz continued: "They're running for he-man, women-haters club or something. That's what they go at. That's not what people are interested in. There is angst. Because robber barons like J. D. Vance and Donald Trump gutted the Midwest, told us we didn't do that. . . . That angst that J. D. Vance talks about in *Hillbilly Elegy*, none of my hillbilly cousins went to Yale, and none of them went on to be venture capitalists or whatever. It's not who people really are. I think that message doesn't resonate."

Within minutes, Walz's tagging Vance as "weird" went viral.

As a born-and-bred western Pennsylvanian, where Appalachian Ohio and West Virginia cultures and traditions overlap with his home state, LaCivita tends to scorn elites who like to toss out people like a throwaway line from *Law and Order*.

These western Pennsylvania voters are the same voters whom Barack Obama, while at a glitzy fundraiser in San Francisco, called "bitter" folks who "cling to guns," resentment, and Bibles.[13]

At an LGBTQ fundraiser in New York City, Hillary Clinton called Trump voters "a basket of deplorables" and without redemption, and that wasn't all she said at that event. She continued by saying these voters are "racist, sexist, homophobic, xenophobic, Islamophobic—you name it."[14] At a Democratic Town Hall in March of 2016 in Columbus, Ohio, she told a group of coal miners that she would put them out of business.[15] Joe Biden loved to call these voters "extremist" on a regular basis.[16]

LaCivita was pretty sure that calling J. D. Vance "weird" would rub people the wrong way. People in places like Appalachian Pennsylvania and Ohio were going to have words.

So would Vance. LaCivita smiled to himself. He was pretty sure the Democrats were going to regret opening this can of worms.

On August 2, *Axios* reported with assurance that all signs pointed to Shapiro becoming Harris's running mate. It was a shrewd and straightforward move, according to a variety of sources, both Republican and Democrat.

Manuel Bonder, Shapiro's spokesperson, had told me the day before that Shapiro had canceled a scheduled trip to the Hamptons that would have included a meet-and-greet with donors and fundraisers for his campaign. The news media were convinced that Shapiro would soon be on the presidential ticket. I had my doubts. He and Harris were not a good fit. Shapiro is a talented political athlete—I've known him for decades and covered him for as long, and this is a guy who is no one's second. His style and character are too different from hers, and if there were doubts that Biden could win, there were even more doubts that she could win Pennsylvania.

Shapiro met with Harris on Sunday. She announced to the world two days later that her choice was Walz. Shapiro told me the day after the Philadelphia rally that "Harris had a deeply personal decision to make about who she wanted to be a running mate. . . . And in the end, I had a deeply personal decision to make as well."

It was clear, at least to me, that he did not want the job.

In Philadelphia two days earlier, Walz did two things that made LaCivita privately happy. Something was off about his alternating bowing toward Harris and theatrical applause during her speech. But it wasn't just that. LaCivita had a gut feeling that Walz's decision to call Vance "creepy, and yeah, just weird as hell" would come back to bite the candidates.

People don't take kindly to their type being called weird.

Chapter 7

The Return

I want to introduce you to a person. One of the most talented writers. A person who truly has the pulse of this area, Pennsylvania, and the Rust Belt in general. The Rust Belt is her territory. Nobody covers it better. Salena Zito! Salena, where are you, Salena? Where are you? Thank you! She is a great writer.

—Donald J. Trump, July 31, 2024, to a packed house of supporters in Harrisburg

Donald Trump was ten minutes into his speech at the New Holland Arena in the Farm Show Complex, and I was gone—twenty-two miles away, to be exact, heading home on US 22 with my daughter Shannon Venditti—when my phone started blowing up with texts. My daughter began to read them to me, but they were coming in so fast, she could hardly keep up with them. There were hundreds, from people on the Trump team, rally-goers, and people watching the rally on C-SPAN, all telling me that the president had just mentioned me on stage.

Oh boy, I thought.

Trump had told me to stick around, but we had a three-hour drive looming, the wireless service in the arena was nonexistent, and I had to get home and write the story about our interview.

I glanced at Shannon, and we burst out laughing. Our laughter got out of hand, sort of like when an *SNL* guest breaks character during a skit. Soon tears were running down our faces. "How is this your life?" she asked for the hundredth time in the past eighteen days. I reminded her how awkward I am with receiving attention and that it would have been worse if I had been there.

"What are you going to tell them?" Shannon asked.

"Tell them I was in the bathroom," I told her to text people.

"Of course, the bathroom. Good call. Everyone will believe that," she said, and we started laughing again until it dawned on me that there was something Shannon didn't know.

"Actually, Trump knows I don't like public bathrooms," I admitted.

Shannon looked at me incredulously. Of course *she* knows that; I am her mother, and she has traveled with me all of my life, but *how in the heck would he know that?*

Shannon gave me *that look.*

I quickly explained that in May of 2020, I had interviewed Trump at an event in Allentown, Pennsylvania, one day after his "15 Days to Slow the Spread" (which had actually been more like six weeks) mandate had lifted. The event had been held at Owens & Minor, one of five companies in the nation selected by the Department of Health and Human Services to supply 600 million N95 respirator masks to hospitals and surgical centers and a good five-and-a-half-hour drive from home.

After the interview concluded, Trump began chatting with me, asking me about what it had been like during the shutdowns. He eventually asked what the drive was like as I crossed the state: "Did you see a lot of people on the road?" he asked, genuinely hopeful that the country was starting to get back to normal.

He asked about gas stations being open. "They are, sir," then for God knows whatever reason, I admitted to the president of the United States that I wasn't a big fan of public restrooms. What the heck was I thinking?

Trump gave me a look. "How far of a drive is it from Pittsburgh?"

"Six hours or so."

"You drink Coke? Coffee?"

"Yup. Coffee."

I thought I knew what he wanted to ask next, so I took the leap and told him a quick Dolly Parton story I had once heard, something to the effect that sometimes you just have to pee off the back of a truck.

"Did you just say you went off the side of a truck?" he asked, clearly amused by the story I just backed myself into.

I said, "Of course not. I drive a Jeep."

Trump looked at me. Then we both laughed. A lot. It had been a long six weeks of being cooped up, first for the initial two weeks of the stop the spread mandate, which was extended to six weeks, based on the then-CDC's recommendations to stay home to help prevent spread of COVID.

Shannon looked at me, incredulous. "*Who are you?*" she asked. We both started laughing all over again as the texts continued to burn up my phone.

———

Harrisburg, Pennsylvania (fourteen hours earlier)

It was nearly dawn when I drove across US 22 on Wednesday, July 31. It had been eighteen days since President Donald Trump was shot in Butler, Pennsylvania; sixteen days since he announced J. D. Vance as his running mate; thirteen days since he gave his acceptance speech at the Republican National Convention in Milwaukee; ten days since Joe Biden decided to end his run for reelection and endorse Vice President Kamala Harris as the Democratic nominee; and eight days since Secret Service director Kimberly Cheatle resigned as a result of Trump's near assassination.

Everything about the presidential campaign was centered on Pennsylvania. Governor Josh Shapiro was being considered as Harris's vice-presidential pick, and voters reacting to Trump being shot in their home state had come out of the woodwork in support of him. Seemingly overnight, people were no longer afraid to place a Trump sign in their yard or fly a Trump flag. I saw signs where I expected to see them, in the more rural areas, but I also saw them in the predominantly Black neighborhoods of Pittsburgh. I saw them in working-class Philadelphia. I saw them spring up in affluent suburban enclaves where supposedly Trump was losing voters, if one believed the "experts."

People began to wear their Trump gear again in public, including the iconic Make America Great Again hats. A lot of young people—*a lot*—were engaged in supporting Trump across the state. The press seemed to overlook the number of young women, Black Americans, and Asian and Hispanic voters who had also come out to support Trump. The Democrats were focused on abortion access, as if it were the only thing they believed people would vote on. They simply weren't listening to these voters.

The weekend before July 31, Krissy Eckenrode, a young mother and college-educated professional from Mt. Lebanon, stood on the sidelines of a suburban Pittsburgh soccer field, watching her daughter's game. She wore a Trump hat, the red one that everyone recognizes, and a huge smile.

"Two weeks ago, I would have hidden that I am a Trump supporter," she confessed. "The comments were too much. Well, not
anymore. If he can take a bullet, surely, I can wear a hat and take
whatever judgment I get from others with a spine."

This sentiment became a common theme that I reported over
and over again. Yet few other reporters seemed to notice. According to the tone-deaf press, Eckenrode was supposed to be a Harris voter—she was part of a widening gender gap. *Her husband is
telling her how to vote* would soon become the narrative in news
stories, social media memes, and numerous ads with Hollywood
actresses whispering that it is "okay not to tell your husband how
you will vote."

People in the press echoed this as if it was a real thing. Why
were they getting this so wrong?

The answer is simple. Most members of the national press—
like all cultural curators in US corporations, academia, institutions
like public policy think tanks, Hollywood, and government—live,
work, and socialize in the same ten counties surrounding Washington, DC, or in New York City. These locations are centers of
wealth and power, and all of their residents, including a press corps
supposed to dispassionately cover the presidential race, have little
in common with voters outside of these areas.

They often report on people who regularly attend church or
make faith an important part of their lives, people who own guns
and know how to shoot them, people who are pro-life. These
reporters equate intelligence with college degrees because everyone they know has a college degree, everyone they socialize with
has a college degree—heck, anyone who is successful, in their
minds, has a college degree.

Yet they are covering news about people who hold very different values than theirs. Neither outlook is right or wrong, but as a

reporter, if you do not understand who you are covering or at least some aspect of cultural connections, and if you're not open to people's differences, your reporting will come across as if you had landed on an alien planet and are describing the species you encounter. Or your reporting will drip with condescending adjectives.

When Trump took office in 2017, national news organizations made a feeble attempt to cover the middle of the country. I was brought on with CNN as a contributor to give a different worldview, and within a week, I was being asked questions about Russia, an area in which I had zero expertise. Rather than asking questions about why voters in Pennsylvania saw things as they did, reporters asked why voters in Pennsylvania were "racist."

It quickly became popular to criticize journalists, including me, for spending too much time reporting about places that used to be something much greater—places like Butler, Johnstown, and Wilkes-Barre in Pennsylvania, to name a few. For me, that was a problem. I live in Pennsylvania. Luckily, CNN used me less and less, and by the end of my tenure five years later, I could count on one hand the number of times I went on air in 2020.

The press had become bored with and ultimately dismissive of places that once prospered, and the people who made them thrive, by the time the 2024 election cycle began. The reporting went from being tinged with mild annoyance to full-on hostility, with stories and quips on social media that blamed the collapse of these places on some sort of racism, denialism, or lack of intelligence among the populace.

Such reports overlooked the complexities of the impact on communities of bad trade deals, automation, and the delocalization of business headquarters.

Worse, elitist reporters and others clearly blamed the people who had put Trump in office the first time and might just do it again. They miscalculated how much their perspective insulted these voters and potential new voters regarding their sense of place in society.

Tom Maraffa, a geography professor at Youngstown State University, explained it to me this way: "Placeless people, like those highly critical of fly-over folks, develop affinities for ideology and abstractions, as opposed to neighborhoods and cities. The lives of the coastal elites, academics, big-business owners, high-tech innovators, entertainers, and media personalities have led to this because they are so mobile."

The people who came to see Trump in Butler had come from a long line of families who were intentionally not mobile. According to US Census data, seven in ten people in Pennsylvania live within just a few miles of where they grew up.[1] The proximity to family, traditions, and a way of life were more important to them than upward mobility and a nice bonus check.

Neither the rooted nor the rootless is "better" than the other. But too often, the cultures clash, with one spending an inordinate amount of time putting the other down, usually on a widely read platform.

"Most people in places across Pennsylvania, Ohio, Michigan, and Wisconsin, in small towns, rural areas, and some cities, are tied to their places for generations. So, issues such as climate change and globalization are therefore viewed fundamentally differently," Maraffa explained.

As Shannon and I headed to Harrisburg, it was just past 6:00 a.m., and the sun was edging over the horizon. We were going to cover Trump's return to the state of Pennsylvania.

It would be our first rally since the assassination attempt that put us in the crosshairs. After we parked, we took a walk along North Cameron Street. In the distance, we could see the golden pink light inching its way over the Capitol dome from the outside of the Farm Show Complex where Trump would give his first speech in Pennsylvania since being shot.

Despite the early hour, nine-year-old Colton Ream was beaming as he walked with his parents. Actually, he was skipping, holding their hands while straining to see the colorful avenue of vendor booths ahead. Flags fluttered and balloons bounced in the air, and the booths were filled with patriotic merchandise. A line of people wrapped around the complex. The Ream family said they had left their Annville home before dawn to bring their son to his first Trump rally.

The energy was palpable. It was already hot outside, predicted to reach 90 degrees Fahrenheit by noon, but that didn't affect the crowd's anticipation.

The significance of where Trump would hold his first Pennsylvania rally since Butler wasn't mentioned by the national media or even the local press—perhaps they did not comprehend the emotional weight that having the rally at the New Holland Arena would mean to people across the state.

But it was not lost on those of us standing in the line along North Cameron Street. Traffic inched slowly along US 22, the main artery into town, backed up for over two miles in either direction. Drivers would fill the designated parking spots by noon for an event not scheduled to start for another six hours.

The Pennsylvania Farm Show Complex is meaningful not just to the people who live in Dauphin County but to many throughout the state. Agriculture is the eighth-largest employer in Pennsylvania. Even more meaningful is the New Holland Arena where Trump was set to speak. The arena was named after a local farm supply company that holds significance to those involved in agriculture—a leading industry that puts $132.5 billion annually into the state's economy—because of what happens in the arena every year.

Pacing up and down North Cameron Street was Chris Herr, executive vice president of Pennsylvania's largest agricultural trade organization. He marveled at Trump's genius for choosing the New Holland Arena for his event.

Herr is a third-generation farmer who, as a youngster, won his fair share of 4-H blue ribbons here, including some for shearing and for his livestock. The arena is sacred to many, he explained.

"The dirt floor of this arena is where the horse pull competitions are held, as well as the high school rodeo, which, by the way, is the second-largest high school rodeo event in the country," Herr said. "It is also where the cattle competition is held for the 4-H. Just about everything from square dancing to tractor square dancing happens here, attracting farmers young and old from across the state."

Every January, this complex fills with farmers and people in agriculture from all sixty counties for the annual Pennsylvania Farm Show. Agribusiness has been central to the state's culture and economy since its early days as a colony, thanks to the Appalachian Mountains and the seemingly endless miles of farm fields, orchards, and forests. It has shaped the state's economy and its identity for centuries.

The voters filling this place several hours before Trump would even step on the stage are people emotionally tied to this election cycle. They are also emotionally tied to place—it was a farm show complex in Butler where Trump had been shot, and it was a farm show complex here in Dauphin County where he would return.

Many attendees showed their first hogs here, participated in their first rodeos, danced their first high step, or perhaps even asked their best girl to marry them in the stands during a competition.

When you think about how many great things have happened at this arena, Herr said, it shows that Trump understood the significance of place when choosing a location for his rally. "That is why he picked Butler. That is why he picked here."

Just how important is agriculture to Pennsylvania? The state is home to more than three thousand farms on 7.3 million acres, accounting for $83.8 billion in direct economic output. But for the past four years, the industry has been hurting. When inflation began skyrocketing in mid-2021 and fertilizer costs for farmers exploded with a whopping 300 percent price increase by 2022, it was farmers who absorbed the costs just in purchasing alone.

And when Pennsylvania farmers bristled at escalating energy costs, no one in Washington listened. President Joe Biden seemed to be tone-deaf. He said inflation was "temporary" while his administration insisted it was "transitory."[2] Then he said they had it all wrong, and that "Bidenomics" was working. Kamala Harris was equally tone-deaf. The dismissal of these two politicians led farmers to blame the ideological decisions made by a government both culturally and geographically distanced from farming communities.

Similarly, the Biden-Harris administration seemed not to understand the symmetry between farmers and the natural gas industry in Pennsylvania.

The administration's efforts to stop fossil fuel pipeline construction from day one and to close existing supply lines wreaked havoc on the price of supplies for farmers. When Biden decided in early 2024 to ban the export of liquid natural gas, rural farming voters, as well as union voters, broke with the president. That moratorium impacted not only union jobs in the energy industry but also farmers who relied on royalties from gas wells on their property to help keep their family farms going.

Shannon and I were scheduled to interview Trump that day. My first questions were going to be on energy and farming, and then we'd talk about how he was doing.

By 2:00 p.m., the line was twenty people across and miles long— literally, miles. Shannon and I made our way to the press entrance and slipped into the arena. The doors had just opened, and the arena was already half full, with a lot of people still outside.

Cindy Foust and her husband Denny were two of the first people to settle into their seats just above the press riser after the gates opened.

Cindy is a retired banker; Denny is a retired CPA and current president of the nine-thousand-member international Studebaker Drivers Club. They said they came to hear the former president lay out what he would do to help improve their lives and communities.

"It's not talked about with enough seriousness, how much inflation has impacted families' budgets," Cindy said, as Denny nodded in agreement. "That is what I like about Trump. He talks to us about us, and I want to hear how he will make our lives better."

Trump arrived at the arena around 5:40 p.m., heading first to a holding area called the "click room" behind the stage, draped off in a blue curtain on all sides. Secret Service agents surrounded the curtained-off area along with a group of Pennsylvania State Police troopers.

The campaign's advance press staffer directed Shannon and me to a line just outside the curtained-off section. At the front of the line were elected officials: Pennsylvania Republican representatives Mike Kelly, Scott Perry, Lloyd Smucker, John Joyce, and Dan Meuser as well as Republican Senate candidate Dave McCormick.

We felt like proverbial flies on the wall. Someone, I cannot remember who, said, "The president wants to see you." Then I heard from inside the tent, "Salena? Where is my Salena?" Shannon looked at me, "*Who are you, seriously?*"

The press staffer brought us into the room. There was Trump, with an American flag behind him, and he was talking with a local elected official I recognized but couldn't recall her name. Photographers were amassed across from him.

Chris LaCivita peeked through the curtain. "Salena!" We hugged. Although we have interacted over the years by phone, I had not seen him in person since the blistering summer day in 2006 when I went to Winchester, Virginia, to interview his then-client Senator George Allen and he insisted that I conduct the interview on a horse. It was a test. I passed. I hopped up on that horse, dress and all, and did the interview. We have been friends ever since.

We also bonded over our western Pennsylvania roots. Shannon snapped a photo of us and sent it off to Brad Todd, my coauthor on *The Great Revolt: Inside the Populist Coalition Reshaping American Politics*, the 2018 bestseller that dove headfirst into the new conservative coalition long before most analysts and reporters even scratched the surface of the tectonic shift happening within the middle class.

"Salena, Salena! Where are you? I want you over here." I could hear Trump calling out from behind me. LaCivita looked at me and laughed. Shannon and I eased our way behind the cameras, but Trump was having none of that.

"Come over here where I can see you," he said, pointing for me to stand beside campaign cochair Susie Wiles and Margo Martin, who has been the former president's press assistant since he was first in the White House. Elegant, sweet, and always in command of the situation surrounding Trump, the twenty-eight-year-old Martin is now his deputy director of communications.

Shannon stayed with the camera crew. "Who is that? Is that your daughter?" Trump said. "Shannon, come over here too." He pointed to where I stood.

"Look at you, Shannon," he continued. "Both of you, come over here and get your photo taken. You know, Shannon, your mom is the best—*the best*. No one knows the voters better than her.

"Also, she has the best hair. Best hair in journalism," he joked.

Everyone in the room began to laugh, and I wanted to crawl under a rock. LaCivita whispered to me, *"You hate attention, don't you?"*

Now we truly were flies on the wall, watching the dignitaries pay their respects. The "real people" started coming through the line, about four dozen of them, mostly families and locals, but also local law enforcement officers, first responders, and veterans of wars from Vietnam through Iraq and Afghanistan. It was then that I got a glimpse of Trump in a way that few reporters do.

He was generous with his hugs and lingering handshakes with each person who had stood in line to see him. He asked them about their lives and where they lived, and he hugged them and shook their hands again.

So much for the Purell presidency, I thought, remembering the many stories about his germaphobia by reporters who said he would slather his hands with sanitizer after each handshake. I saw none of that. *More people should see this side of him*, I thought.

The meet-and-greet took a little too long for the event's planners, but it was interesting to watch and to listen to the conversations between Trump and Pennsylvanians whose accomplishments rarely rise to the forefront of conversations beyond their families.

Trump moved Shannon and me into another curtained-off room to sit on a gray couch for an interview. We were directly behind the stage, and the chorus of ABBA's "Dancing Queen" was echoing throughout the arena. It had been eighteen days since we last saw each other, seventeen days since we had spoken, a conversation related to the assassination attempt.

"I feel good," Trump said now. When I pressed him, he took my hand. He didn't want to talk about the shooting.

Just a few feet away, the crowd roared as the anticipation grew. I asked him if he won in November, what would he tell the people four years from now that he delivered for them in his second term?

"I think more than anything else, hope. Because the people of this country have no hope," he said, ticking off a list of problems that have affected people's lives that he links directly to Biden-Harris policies.

"Inflation, the border, crime, the ability to buy a home—they [people] don't have the American dream anymore," he said. "I'm going to be talking about it in my speech tonight, about how we achieve that."

He said he wants restoring the American dream to be his legacy.

Outside the event, the national media were talking about Trump's interview in Chicago during the National Association of Black Journalists (NABJ) convention. The consensus was that he bombed it; these reporters seemed consumed with the story to the exclusion of everything happening in front of them. They were missing the real story.

Trump told me he saw his visit to the NABJ convention differently.

"I showed up," he said, pointing out that despite the strained back and forth, it was something his Democratic opponent, Kamala Harris, did not do. So why does he show up in places where people don't expect him to? He goes to the Bronx, New Jersey, Temple University in Philadelphia, and Detroit—places where no Republican candidate, even he, has earned even token support in decades.

Trump explained that this was no different from his decision in 2016 to show up in places like Ashtabula, Ohio; Luzerne, Pennsylvania; and Kent County, Michigan—places Republican and Democratic presidential campaigns rarely visited over the years, let alone held rallies. He said that because the middle class is the beating heart of the country, this election is about restoring prosperity and hope to middle-class America everywhere in the nation.

"These are incredible people," he said of the firefighters, laborers, construction workers, and small businessmen and women who are among those making up the middle class.

"These are the ones that built our country—people like Corey Comperatore, they work their asses off, and they built this country," he said of the former fire chief and Army Reservist who lost his life at the Butler rally from one of the shooter's bullets. I asked Trump whether he thinks Corey's life of hard work, volunteerism, and devotion to family represent the voters who support him.

He nodded yes.

The typical Trump playlist was getting close to his entrance theme song. He was seeking to energize supporters again. Two weeks ago, Trump was ahead in polling against Biden. One week ago, Harris became the party's nominee, and the national press claimed she had closed the polling gap. I was not convinced. It was being reported more vigorously that Governor Shapiro would likely be named her running mate. I was not convinced of that, either.

What was true was that Harris was enjoying robust attention from the press, as was Shapiro. It was unclear if that mattered to voters anymore, though. Trump had no intention of letting her gain momentum. So, despite his preference for showmanship—he *really* loves a good show—Trump acknowledged the race would come down to who can connect better with voters and talk about them *to them*.

He was adamant that he would hit Harris hard on fracking, and we talked about the impact the liquefied natural gas export ban had on farmers. As I got up to leave, he paused at a table displaying a comb and a can of hairspray.

"Salena, do you use hairspray?"

"Oh no, Mr. President, my hair is big enough that I don't need that."

"Salena—you should try it," he said and aimed the can toward my hair. I wiggled away. He sprayed at my hair, and everyone, including me, was in stitches. Then he told me he had one more thing to say.

"We're going to say what we're going to do because we're going to bring back the country. Harris can't bring back the country," Trump said, serious now as he made his way toward the stage.

He walked out of the curtained room, and we all joined him. He shook hands with all the Secret Service agents and state troopers standing at the arena entrance. He looked back at me: "Hey, you are going to be in there, right? Margo, make sure she has a seat. You'll be in there, right?"

I nodded yes.

Shannon and I were escorted out of the backstage area and back to the press riser. She took some photos as Lee Greenwood's "Proud to be an American" started to blare over the loudspeakers and Trump walked out onto the stage. The energy in the room was overwhelming. I opened my laptop and discovered that the wireless connection was useless.

"We have to go," I told Shannon. "I can't write in here, and I have a story that needs to go up." We made our way out to the car and soon were on the road, heading home.

Twenty-two miles into the ride, the texts started burning up my phone.

Chapter 8

The Son of Appalachia

NORTH PHILADELPHIA, Pennsylvania

The drive across Pennsylvania from Westmoreland County in the early morning hours of August 6 wasn't just beautiful; it was instructive. I took the backroads, mostly along US 30, the iconic Lincoln Highway, the country's first coast-to-coast "highway," which opened in 1913.

Most of the route is still intact as it was designed 111 years earlier. Drivers pass through small towns, farmland, and midsized postindustrial cities. Many of these places were left behind decades ago after the interstate system was built as a faster alternative to US 30—the Pennsylvania Turnpike had the biggest impact on the small businesses and people "left behind."

Thanks to the speed and efficiency of the interstate system, families no longer drove along US 30's winding, often narrow two-lane asphalt looking for roadside attractions to entertain them, like the "World's Largest Coffee Pot" in Bedford. Nor did they stay at tourist motor court cottages like the Lincoln Motor Court along the Somerset-Bedford County line or eat at a family-owned diner. They no longer had to wait at stop signs, traffic lights, or railroad crossings as a freight train's slow chugging held up intersections. Today's travelers are in a rush, and the interstates provide speed as well as access to chain hotels and fast-food restaurants at the interchanges.

But the backroads drive provides a kaleidoscope of Pennsylvania's riches—and it serves as a microcosm of rural America in terms of culture, pace, values, and way of life. If you understand the voters of Indiana, Cambria, Erie, Luzerne, Somerset, Bedford, York, Bucks, and Lancaster Counties of Pennsylvania, well, then you really understand what is going on in the country.

On this day, I saw a flurry of Trump-Vance signs along the highway, many of them homemade, which demonstrates a different level of enthusiasm than going down to the local Republican headquarters and picking up the standard sign. There were scores of homemade "Fight! Fight! Fight!" signs, a hat tip to Trump's reaction after he was shot weeks earlier.

Yes, there were the occasional Harris signs. I remembered what Brad Todd, my friend and coauthor of *The Great Revolt*, told me: "Signs don't vote." Okay, I won't get ahead of my skis regarding what I think is happening . . . for now.

My original destination was the north Philadelphia neighborhood of Cecil B. Moore for Kamala Harris's first campaign rally as the Democrats' nominee. She was holding it at the Liacouras Center where she would not only officially kick off her presidential campaign but also announce her vice-presidential pick.

I had just passed Gettysburg and was entering the little village of New Oxford where I planned to grab a coffee at my favorite coffee shop, Deja Brew, when CNN broke the news on SiriusXM that Harris had chosen Minnesota governor Tim Walz and not Pennsylvania governor Josh Shapiro to be her running mate.

CNN reported that Harris gave Walz the news on a video call and that he would join her at Liacouras, the ten-thousand-seat basketball arena on the Temple University campus. Just two months earlier, Donald Trump held his first-ever rally in Philadelphia at the same space.

At the time of the Trump event, I reported that the former president had a keen understanding of "place," and that was why he held a rally in Philadelphia. Was he going to win the majority of the city's votes? Of course not. However, it was important to show he was willing to go places where Republicans traditionally don't try to earn votes—Democrats outnumber Republicans seven-to-one in Philly. Trump, Chris LaCivita, Susie Wiles, and Tony Fabrizio knew the coalition was changing incrementally; however, few in the press had caught on.

A headline in the *Philadelphia Inquirer* proved my point: "Why Is Donald Trump Coming to North Philadelphia for His First-Ever Rally in the City."

Manuel Bonder, the governor's press secretary, called to tell me that Shapiro would join Walz and Harris at the campaign event. Shapiro texted me that he would be giving a speech at the event.

Just two days earlier Shapiro, Walz, and Senator Mark Kelly separately had been at Harris's residence at the US Naval Observatory in Washington, DC, interviewing for the job. Shapiro entered and left the interview with the same sentiment: he wasn't ready to leave his job as governor of Pennsylvania.

I flipped the radio among MSNBC, CNN, and NPR and listened as media members gushed over the Walz pick, with accolades about his folksiness, military service, Midwest pragmatism, and, my favorite accolade of all, "He looks and talks like a lot of the voters we've lost to Trump," which came from a "longtime Democratic operative" on a CNN segment.

My first reaction was: *They don't get it.* Walz is a guy who looks and talks like *what they think a Trump voter looks and talks like*, but you don't just slap plaid on a person and have them say "aw shucks" a couple of times and expect them to share your values.

By sheer happenstance, I covered Walz when he first ran for Congress in 2006. He was one of several Democratic House candidates I covered in the Midwest states whom I had identified as capable of flipping the House majority for the first time since 1994. This was during President George W. Bush's last midterm election cycle, and Walz was running against longtime Republican congressman Gil Gutknecht for a conservative suburban Missouri district as an "aw shucks" guy. Voters that cycle were angry at the Republican Party for the prolonged wars and the expansion of government under their watch—so they voted *against* Republicans, not *for* Democrats. This occurred not only in a conservative Minnesota district but also in three seats in Pennsylvania that I covered.

That voter irritation with a party's direction is a nuance few understand, yet it happens almost every "wave" cycle, with whoever wins the congressional majority thinking everybody loves their party now and they have a mandate, when in actuality, voters just applied the brakes.

By 2016, Walz had moved from "folksy" with an endorsement from the National Rifle Association (NRA) to a candidate who barely won that cycle; in 2018, he looked at the tea leaves, denounced the NRA, embraced progressivism, and announced he would seek the office of governor.

The mask was off.

The press hailed him as "Minnesota nice." It had been eighteen years since I covered his congressional race, and I did not remember having that sentiment. Pennsylvania Democratic media strategist Larry Ceisler, a friend of Shapiro's, called me to ask what I thought of Harris's choice, pointing out all the accolades the press was pumping out. "Look, the guy seems relatable. I think he is going to do great in those rural areas of Erie, Lancaster, and Luzerne that you write about in the middle of our state," he said.

"Just because a person wears plaid does not mean they are nice," I told him.

Ceisler said everyone loves a high school football coach, and I cautioned him right there—both of my kids were high-achieving high school athletes, my daughter Shannon in soccer and my son Glenn in football, so trust me, high school coaches being beloved is not always true.

"Not every football coach is the 'grumpy but lovable Wilford Brimley' in *The Natural*," I reminded him. "High school sports are not a Hollywood movie."

I had found Walz's constant use of "weird" thrown at J. D. Vance to be peculiar; however, it certainly got him attention. Since he first said it on TV, on July 23 after Harris was named as the Democrats' replacement for Joe Biden, this characterization of Vance spread through edited clips of him acting "weird." The news media began calling him "weird." So did Harris. So did Senator Joe Manchin (D-WV). In fact, almost every panelist on MSNBC and CNN called Vance and Trump weird.

The Associated Press even reported that the "Vance is weird" message provided Democrats with a "narrative advantage," without asking a single voter outside of New York and Washington, DC, if it actually did.[1]

As I headed toward the Liacouras Center that day, I decided it would be more interesting to cover Vance than Harris. He was holding his first rally at the 2300 Arena, which was five miles from the Liacouras Center. I changed my Google Maps destination, looked at my watch, and tapped the gas pedal. I still had plenty of time to get there by noon.

I was going to see what people thought of the "weird" guy.

I first heard of J. D. Vance when I read his book *Hillbilly Elegy* on June 1, 2016. This was twenty-nine days before the book gained national attention after *New York Times* columnist David Brooks recommended it as a way to understand the typical Trump voter in an article headlined: "Revolt of the Masses: Cultivating New Patriotism."[2]

Within weeks, seemingly every reporter, book reviewer, and cable TV news host was writing about or referring to Vance's book as the decoder to understanding the Trump voter. By January of 2017, both Vance and I were contributors on CNN. The network chose me because of my reporting throughout that cycle and because I understood the changing party coalitions and that Trump was going to win. Vance was chosen because, as a Yale University grad and now venture capitalist, he had made it out—he had become the elites' bridge between Trump voters and themselves.

We met during the lead-up to Trump's inauguration in January 2017, when we locked eyes over one panelist's comments about the "intellect" of Trump voters. Vance and I came from the same place—he grew up in a dying steel town in Ohio, and I was from one in Pennsylvania.

After the segment, we introduced ourselves. I gushed over the book, not because it was a decoder but because it rang true to a world I grew up around. I may have been from the largest city in Appalachia, but the culture and experiences were very similar.

He complimented my reporting; both of us agreed that we were already weary of the constant Trump voter–bashing.

We never worked together on another panel, and Vance left CNN shortly after that. We didn't see each other again until April 2018, when he and I did an event together in Raleigh, North Carolina, titled "Hillbilly Elegy and the Urban-Rural Divide."

The event, hosted by the Carolina Partnership for Reform—a public benefit think tank focused on research and education on conservative policy reforms—was basically an onstage conversation, and it was packed to the rafters with hundreds of young people. I left feeling deeply impressed by this young man. I told him he would be governor of Ohio one day; he laughed.

I next saw him in November 2021 in Steubenville, Ohio, wearing a dapper navy-blue suit and holding a Big Gulp–sized drink while talking to about a hundred people gathered at Leonardo's Coffeehouse and sampling an ample supply of Ohio Valley–style pizza, a square pie known for its light but crunchy dough, sweet sauce, and cold shredded cheese.

Vance was now a candidate—not for governor, as I had told him four years earlier, but for the Republican Party nomination for the US Senate seat that would be open due to the retirement of Republican Rob Portman. There were six candidates in that race, and he was in third place.

He had only three months to turn things in his favor, but I stopped wondering if he could do that when he started talking to the voters: "I grew up in a town not too different from Steubenville . . . a steel-mill town like this one," he said, adding that it was his grandparents who raised him.[3]

He was connecting.

"My mom struggled with opioid addiction for a big part of my early childhood, so Mamaw and Papaw were really the people that provided me stability and comfort. And one of the things that makes me really sad is a lot of these small towns across the state ... were decimated by very stupid decisions to move our manufacturing base to China."

Yeah, this guy is relatable, I thought. I saw it in the reactions of the people who came to "kick the tires." They didn't see his suit, they saw the Big Gulp of Mountain Dew, heard the soft twang of his Midwest accent, and listened to his story. He *saw* them, many of the voters there told me. *He might pull this off*, I thought. And a few months later, Trump had endorsed him over the other five Senate contenders, a move that shocked the press, who pointed to Vance's criticizing the former president's comportment in 2016. They couldn't understand how Trump could endorse someone who didn't care for his "outside-the-box" rhetoric. They couldn't understand how Vance could support Trump, either.

The *Atlantic*, the premier news magazine for the elite class, was furious. David Graham penned a piece that basically called Vance a traitor to his class, saying he had become a cultural heroin dealer.[4] *My God, he went to Yale—what could Graham be thinking*, I wondered.

It was clear to me, once again, that many of my colleagues don't really know a single Trump voter. Why? Well, a good many of his voters don't like Trump's comportment but still vote for him. Others went from not being Trump supporters early on to voting for him.

Vance was just like them. He won the primary overwhelmingly one month after Trump's endorsement. His general election opponent was Tim Ryan, a Niles, Ohio, Democrat who challenged Nancy Pelosi for House leadership after Trump won in 2016 and was once considered moderate and pragmatic. He bewilderingly decided to tack left in the race. Reporters were convinced Ryan would win—so were Democrats and establishment Republicans who also didn't care much for Vance.

One month before the November 2022 general election, I headed to Portage County, Ohio. Suffolk University and *USA Today* had just released a poll showing the Senate race to be a pure toss-up, with Ryan leading Vance by one percentage point.[5] I was skeptical. I had been covering the cycle all summer and fall and had never seen Ryan's popularity surge.

Vance was just about to walk into the sunroom at the Aurora, a refurbished inn in this upper-middle-class suburb located in Portage County between Akron and Cleveland. It was the second of three events in the northeastern counties: he had already stopped in Stark County (Canton), then Mahoning County (Youngstown) the next day for his debate with Ryan.

In the last cycle, Ryan held his congressional seat but lost his home county of Trumbull. For perspective, he won it in 2016 by a whopping fifty-nine percentage points.

No other place in this state—or the country, perhaps—better illustrates what most Democrats, establishment Republicans, and mainstream reporters missed in the political earthquake that has been taking place over the last six years in both parties. The working class, the rooted people who have lived in this country for generations, the Americans who pride themselves on *making* this country have moved right.

Paul Sracic of Youngstown State University told me that that part of Ohio was dark blue in politics because of the deep ties between organized labor and the Democratic Party. The voters' values haven't changed, but the parties have, which is why a Republican candidate for Senate who attended Yale was outperforming a Democrat from Niles, outside Youngstown, where folks used to quip that you were baptized Catholic and a Democrat at birth.

Vance's success was in part, because Vance is a child of Appalachia who enlisted in the Marine Corps, went on to achieve great success among the elites, then returned to his roots to raise his family.

Voters here told me they personally liked Ryan, but they didn't trust him when he told them he was an independent thinker. They knew he would still vote with Senate leader Chuck Schumer and the Democrats on big issues—like the spending bill—that have severely impacted their pocketbooks.

Mark McKinnon was there with his TV crew. The former Republican strategist who was now cocreator, producer, and host of Showtime's *The Circus: Inside the Greatest Political Show on Earth* asked to interview me about the race on camera. I told him it was likely that Vance was on his way to a solid victory because the Rust Belt had changed. He shook his head. I've seen that look before. He didn't believe me. I shrugged.

Two weeks later, Vance won by more than six percentage points—it wasn't even close.

———

I made it to Vance's Philadelphia event just in time. A little over two hundred people were there to see him. Not bad for his first trip to Pennsylvania in arguably hostile territory; there aren't many Republicans in Philadelphia.

He was there for a reason. Harris would be rolling out Walz, and Vance was in the city to give the voters a contrast. Vance began his speech by reinforcing the importance of strong border security and called the situation at the southern US border one of the greatest failures of the Biden-Harris administration. He held nothing back: "Kamala Harris has been such a disastrous vice president of this country that everywhere she goes, chaos and uncertainty follow."[6]

Behind Vance were residents who were impacted by problems caused by the open border—the fentanyl crisis and increased crime. Vance talked about his personal experience with his mom Beverly's battle with addiction as he was growing up in Middletown.

However, opposition research shared with reporters showing Vance joking in a 2021 interview with Tucker Carlson that some prominent female Democrats are "childless cat ladies" had become the media's obsession. For over a week, that phrase was the most-searched story about Vance. CNN did a deep dive, as did NPR, NBC, and *The Hill*. The *Washington Post* did a big think piece.[7] The *Columbus Dispatch* did as well.[8]

Vance opened up the event to questions from the national and local press. When a reporter asked him about his "childless cat ladies" comment, someone in the crowd yelled, "This cat lady loves you!"

Vance smiled, answering her, "I love you too, ma'am."

Then he went on to disarm the issue in a way that showed why Trump picked him to be his vice president: "What I said is very simple. I think American families are good, and government policy should be more pro-family. Now, if the media wants to get offended about a sarcastic remark I made before I even ran for the United States Senate, then the media is entitled to get offended. You know what I'm offended by? I'm offended that normal Americans can't afford grocery prices."

Attendees at the event told me they had two things they wanted to hear Vance address: the border and the economy. The press continued asking questions about cat ladies and Project 2025, the latter something both Vance and Trump have adamantly disavowed involvement with. The voters aimed their frustration at the reporters for not asking questions that had to do with the border, crime, drug overdoses, and the economy.

I headed home.

The question of "is she or isn't she" going to pick Shapiro had been answered. As expected, several hours after Vance's rally Shapiro ripped the bark off the tree in his speech at Liacouras Center. Walz charmed the press, although his speech didn't reach the soaring heights that Shapiro's did. The press tried to ignore that. They blamed an anti-Jewish strain in the party for Shapiro's not being selected. They never once considered that *Shapiro didn't want the job*.

In our interview the next day, Shapiro told me bluntly that Harris had a decision to make, and he had a decision to make as well, about what was best for him.

Harris's choice of Walz was a clear signal that this election cycle would be a get-out-the-base election, rather than the coalition-building effort Democrats might have pursued if Harris had chosen Shapiro as her running mate.

Mike Mikus, a Pennsylvania-based Democratic strategist, was running Malcolm Kenyatta's statewide race for treasurer—his candidate would have to run shoulder to shoulder with Harris to win.

Mikus is very up front in saying he saw this race shaping up to be no different in tone and party building than the one we saw in 2012, when President Barack Obama won reelection.

Mikus, who has helped candidates win statewide Democratic races in Pennsylvania for two decades, explained that in 2008, Obama ran an aspirational race with a message of "Hope and Change" that attracted a sizable number of working-class "New Deal Democrats" to his coalition.

"In 2012, he shed those voters in favor of delivering a new base of Democrats, called the 'Ascendant Coalition,' that had a heavy focus on minorities, suburban college-educated women, and young people. That is what Harris is going for," Mikus said.

That pitch leftward and the divisive rhetoric that accompanied it, however, made Obama the first president since Franklin D. Roosevelt to lose voters in his reelection while still winning overall. In Pennsylvania alone, he shed 286,000 voters from 2008 to 2012.

Subtraction is never good for a party.

The next Democratic nominee, Hillary Clinton in 2016, was unsuccessful, with a similar shift leftward. The former First Lady, who was less likable and trusted than Obama, fell short because many of those legacy New Deal Democrats had folded long term into the Republican Party. President Joe Biden was able to bring just enough of them back in 2020, in large part because of the pandemic, but polling leading up to this cycle showed these voters' disappointment in Biden's left-wing governance.

As a result, these voters were leaning toward Trump. Harris, they were quickly realizing, was further to the left than Biden. Her positions on the economy, energy, the border, and crime were demonstratively left of Biden's policies, and now she had picked a running mate with an equally left-wing record as governor of Minnesota.

Chris Borick, a political science professor at Muhlenberg College in Allentown, Pennsylvania, told me that after the Minnesota governor's pick when Walz was one of four hundred members of Congress, his job was to represent his district, one that was center-right. "His pitch left as he left Congress and ran for governor shows when you are the executive of a state, you can be more true to your political beliefs."

Borick warned me that because of Walz's Will Rogers–like folksiness, people might believe he is a centrist. "In politics, it is often about what you project, with your style, and not always what your policies have been."

The selection of Walz as Harris's running mate created an interesting phenomenon among our cultural curators in the press and corporate America: interest in rural voters.

These are the same rural voters they had disparaged for years, with a variety of colorful adjectives that included "bitter," "clinging to guns and God," "deplorable," "extremists" who are a "threat to democracy," and "weird." Yet now they were part of think pieces about Carhartt overalls, Pennsylvania tuxedos, hunter-orange vests, attending a Grange meeting, joining the 4-H Club, and the joys of turkey hunting—as seen through the lens of Walz.

However, the press's exuberance about Walz's Midwest roots was not applied to Vance, who grew up in Midwest Ohio and Appalachian Kentucky. Walz started a line of attack against Vance, saying it was actually he (Walz) who was the true small-town guy in the race and that he's never known anyone who left small-town America to attend Yale.

In his digs, Walz skipped over the rest of Vance's life story, which included making his way out of a dysfunctional family, joining the military, and eventually returning to settle not far from his hometown, then running for US Senate as a political novice and winning.

The press seemed to miss the story that Vance quite literally embodied the American dream. Walz got little pushback from reporters.

Vance took it in stride. After his first event in Pennsylvania, he left the state for Michigan and then went on to Wisconsin. It was August 7, eighteen days since Harris had become the Democratic nominee for president. She had done zero interviews with anyone in the national news press corps.

Astonishingly, reporters were dismissing that this was problematic or even meaningful. I am not big on "what-about-ism," but it was not lost on me that if any Republican candidate for president—in particular, Donald Trump—went eighteen days without talking to the media, their hair would have spontaneously combusted. It is just a fact. And voters were noticing this complacency in the press corps; voters who had rarely considered voting Republican were looking with clear eyes. There is a bias, and it isn't even close.

Vance now had a press pool accompanying him on his campaign plane. He knew it was becoming an issue among reporters that Harris wasn't talking to the press. You can hear people talk.

At the same time, the Trump campaign was running a string of ads about Harris's most recent interviews, before being named the Democratic nominee, reminding people why she was considered such a disaster.

Vance knew that his "cat lady" remark was still being reported by the press. He was also aware that voters had largely detached themselves from the mainstream press. He had clearly calculated that it was time to make a move. His plane landed at the Chippewa Valley Regional Airport in Wisconsin. He had been in both Pennsylvania and Michigan the day before. On impulse, he casually strode across the tarmac from his plane *Trump Force Two* over to *Air Force Two*, Harris's plane. She was in the state at the same time for a campaign event.

It was like the opening scene in Quentin Tarantino's *Reservoir Dogs*—a few men, including Vance and his Secret Service detail, all wearing dark suits and reflective Ray-Bans, walked over to where Harris's press pool was gathered. She had already left the plane and moved to her motorcade behind them.

She still had not answered one question that her press pool fruitlessly shouted at her.

Vance strode over and quipped that he was trying to get a better look at *Air Force Two* because it's "going to be my plane in a few months."

He smiled.

After a couple of gasps and muffled giggles among the reporters, Vance told them that he was worried they "might get a little lonely" because Harris hadn't answered one question in nearly three weeks.[9]

As he said that, Harris's motorcade could be seen in the background, moving off the tarmac without encountering Vance.

New York Magazine wrote about the moment: "Vance Awkwardly Doesn't Confront Harris on Plane Tarmac,"[10] and *The Daily Beast* wrote: "JD Vance Awkwardly Retreats After Bizarre Attempt to Storm Harris' Empty Plane."[11]

They not only got the logistics wrong; they entirely missed the juice: Vance talked to reporters and was willing to take questions. He was willing to take questions from *her* reporters. They also omitted the fact that Harris was gone by the time Vance approached the plane.

Vance then took questions from the press, just as he did after his events in Pennsylvania and Michigan the day before, and he did so with an unexpected ease. His detractors in the Democratic and Republican Parties as well as in the press expected him to cave after several bumpy first weeks as the vice-presidential nominee during which he navigated the opposition research dump that had stalled his stride.

That day, Vance was poised and confident. He got his groove on. The political athlete I had gotten to know over the past few years was not just meeting the moment; he was now an effective attack dog for the Trump team—an attack dog who could deliver his bite with a smile.

I had seen this potential before.

Vance first rose to the occasion just weeks after being sworn in as a senator. In 2023, just before 9:00 p.m. on February 3, the noise of a train screeching to a halt followed by a large explosion jolted the village of East Palestine, Ohio.

The jolt drew hundreds of villagers out of their beds or off their couches and out into the streets. There they saw dozens of rail cars strewn about like a kid's Tonka trucks; flames and smoke were shooting toward the sky, and the sound of colliding train cars echoed for what seemed like forever.

Miraculously, no one was killed in the derailment that night, but the village, where my great-grandfather John Eyster was born and earned a modest twelve votes in his run for office as a Free Silver Democrat, would be changed forever. In the following days, officials feared the chemicals on the train would be an immediate threat—in particular, the flammable gas vinyl chloride, which causes headaches, dizziness, and, in acute cases of exposure, cancer.

Everyone feared that the massive explosion had sent shrapnel and toxic fumes soaring for miles, so officials evacuated nearly two thousand residents. On February 6, Norfolk Southern officials started a controlled burn that sent a fireball into the sky, with a black mushroom cloud that looked like something out of Chernobyl.

Vance was there immediately. He went right down into one of the contaminated creek beds and was filmed scraping its bottom with a large branch, sending a bloom of chemicals to the surface.

"This is disgusting. The fact that these chemicals are still seeping in the ground is an insult to the people who live in East Palestine," Vance said, standing in the middle of a chemical-drenched tributary. [12]

While other government officials made what many felt were gratuitous visits, I went back repeatedly, as did Vance. He pressed for answers, returned to Washington, and introduced the bipartisan Railway Safety Act, which Democratic senators like John Fetterman of Pennsylvania cosponsored.

In February, he brought President Donald Trump to the accident site, a moment I have often argued was the former president's inflection point, not only securing his primary victory but also giving him a secure advantage over Joe Biden.

Two months later, in April of 2023, I caught up with Vance for a story while he was on a visit to one of the Great Oaks Career Campuses, a Cincinnati trade school located not far from his home. He was there to talk to the young people about choosing a trade for their future.

The first classroom he entered was the surgical technology class, which was in the middle of their final exams. Vance had planned to only observe the class, but when he noticed that one of the students was anxious about having her blood drawn by her classmate, he took off his suit jacket and offered to take her place. The teacher did not object, nor did the student, so he sat down, rolled up his sleeve, and smiled.

To the clearly nervous student about to stick a needle in the arm of a US senator, Vance said quietly, "Don't be nervous. If you have to do it again, it's fine with me. I am here for you until you get it right."[13]

The student got it done on the first jab.

The instructor looked at Vance with a broad smile. "Well, that wasn't something I expected I'd see from you today."

After our interview, we sat in the conference room, catching up. He talked about his kids, and I talked about my grandchildren, who are about the same age. His spokesperson, Luke Schroeder, one of the few good press secretaries on Capitol Hill, was with us. I asked about Vance's decision to endorse Trump a year ahead of the 2024 primaries.

"No-brainer. That one was easy," he said, then he paused and looked at me. "I saw his Truth Social media post calling you a fake news reporter that Trump did about you a couple months ago." We both laughed. "Just so you know, I've been there. I think he'll come around."

It dawned on me that Vance could be Trump's vice-presidential pick in 2024. Impulsively, I asked Vance if he would consider it, then asked Vance and Schroeder if they had talked about it. They both laughed at the questions and then told me where the closest Skyline Chili was to the school.

I saw Vance again several months later on February 3, 2024, one year after the train derailment in East Palestine for another story to mark the moment.[14] Vance pulled up in a pickup. He had driven from DC the night before and spent the night in suburban Pittsburgh. Why? He wanted to stop on the way to pick up donuts from Oram's. If you know anything about the area straddling Beaver County, Pennsylvania, and Columbiana County, Ohio, you know you *have to* get your donuts from Oram's. He climbed out of the truck juggling two oversized boxes of donuts.

The smell of yeast, sugar, and cinnamon filled the air as he passed by me and made his way up a flight of stairs to a local church for a meeting with East Palestine residents.

He knew everyone there by their first names. He'd not only been there numerous times; he had also hosted them in Washington, DC. Vance grabbed a glazed bear claw the size of a football, sat down with his constituents, and asked them for an update.

For over an hour, he took questions, listened to their stories, pressed for details, talked candidly about how sick he felt after his first visits there, and, at the end, hugged a grief-stricken Lonnie

Miller, who had lost her home, her small business, and had barely held onto her marriage since the derailment.

There were no trappings of the US Senate—no black SUV, no driver, no entourage, no scrum of national press as Vance donned a hard hat and protective clothing to tour the derailment site with the Environmental Protection Agency or when he walked through the village talking with people on the streets—it was just him, Schroeder, and a local constituent services staffer.

This is a guy few see. The press calls him a fire-breathing dragon, a Trump-like figure too interested in bluster to get things done. His constituents know otherwise.

––––––

Now it was mid-August and Vance was heading to Erie, Pennsylvania—the city located in most important county to win, not just in Pennsylvania but in the country. Win Erie County, and you win Pennsylvania. Win Pennsylvania, and you will be the next president.

The day before Vance arrived, an August 2021 CNN clip emerged of Kamala Harris saying that she fully supported Biden's Afghanistan policies, which ultimately led to the deaths of thirteen soldiers during the Taliban attack at Abbey Gate in the final days of troop withdrawal.

In the resurfaced clip, Harris said she had been the last person in the room with Biden when the decision was made, and it was a decision Harris pointedly said she was "comfortable with."[15]

At the rally in Erie, Vance said she could "go to hell" for that.[16]

At that moment, Vance had been answering a question from a national reporter from the press riser, something he was now doing at every rally, about an alleged incident that occurred when Trump visited Arlington National Cemetery with the family members of those who were killed in the attack.

While Vance's "go to hell" quip made headlines, all of the other things Vance said that day—and the groundswell of support he received in that very important county—were missed. But they would have helped people understand voters' sentiments toward both tickets.

Before the rally, which was held at Team Hardinger, a logistics and trucking company, I had done a brief interview with Vance. I was waiting for him in the click line, in ninety-seven-degree heat, and I was melting. He came over to me after the last person went through the line and noticed my discomfort.

"Hey, want to take this interview into the motorcade car?" Vance asked. "It is *air-conditioned*," he teased. I was in.

We made our way to the back of Hardinger's followed by a flurry of Secret Service agents, confused about what was going on. He got in one side, and I got in the other, and an agent jumped in the front.

"You good, sir?" the agent asked.

Vance smiled. "We are good." He handed me some chocolate candy. I think it was Milk Duds. I thought back to all the Mountain Dews, donuts, and sweets I've seen him enjoy over the years, and I laughed.

"You really have a sweet tooth, don't you?"

During the interview, I asked him if he felt there was any distribution of fairness over the questions he and Trump get, compared to those that Harris and Walz get and still don't answer.

He talked about the gratitude he has, even being in this place, and the wonder of where he came from, to now being the Republican nominee for vice president.

"I am here, and I've been given this incredible opportunity and I'm going to try to make something of it. And the way to make something of it is to actually get out there and talk to people. And yeah, sometimes mediated through a really hostile press but I am not going to sit here and whine and complain because somebody asked me a tough question. There are still a lot of people who are going to hear the answer," he said

He threw back some more chocolate. So did I. I had done what I often do when out on the road, forgotten to eat.

"You can think the question was totally bullshit, but people are still going to hear my answer and that is the cool thing. It is very amazing to know that I get to make this case directly to the American people, and you should take every opportunity you get," he said, adding that he had no plan to not talk to the press.

It was a mantra he sustained throughout the next two months, eventually doing 152 television and print interviews from the time he was named as the nominee until Election Day, a number that didn't include dozens of additional press conferences at rallies and gaggles with his traveling press corps.

He told me his biggest surprise so far on the campaign trail had been the response to his mother, who joined him for appearances from time to time.

"So yesterday, Mom came on the campaign trail with me, and we went to Michigan. We were in Big Rapids, and then we went to Nashville for a fundraiser. And Mom, if you know her—I wish she was with us today because you'd love her—anyway, she has a bit of an R-rated sense of humor, so we had a lot of fun on the airplane. And Mom is a very fun person to be around, so we had a good time," he began.

His face lit up as he talked about her. Clearly, this is a son who loves his mother, even more so for the painful life journey she has made.

"But we go to this A&W root beer stand at Big Rapids, one of the places that's open six months out of the year, because the other six months out of the year it's way too cold," he continued. "And the very first person wants to give my mom a hug, and it's like, 'You are such an inspiration, and a lot of us have struggled with addiction and the fact that you and your son kept at it, that is an inspiration.'"

His eyes welled up, but he regained control of his emotions.

"I think there is, when you come from a non-traditional or non-conventional background, I think there's a certain tendency to want to hide it a little bit and to not tell the story. And obviously, I told the story in *Hillbilly Elegy*, but even then, you don't necessarily want to talk about it so much because it feels uncomfortable. You realize that there are a lot of people who take—not even from my story, but from my mom's story—take some inspiration from that."

His eyes welled up again, but he was smiling.

"And that is definitely something that I've learned, and it has been a very cool thing to watch it unfold," he said.

As we were about to leave his vehicle, Vance, very much like a kid, said, "Tap those windows. They are bulletproof."

Vance drew a big crowd in Erie, three times the size of the one in North Philly. His speech was centered on the dignity of work, and it connected so well with those in attendance that one woman wondered out loud where the heck his Teleprompter was, to which Vance quipped, "Ma'am, I don't need a Teleprompter. I've actually got thoughts in my head, unlike Kamala Harris."[17]

Vance was heading to an off-the-record site, Gordon's Butcher Shop, with the national press. I got to tag along in the press van. I saw several reporters I know, including one from the *New York Times*. We chatted about pleasantries and then he settled in, looking at his phone. They were all looking at their phones. No one was looking up. I mentioned out loud, to no one in particular, the importance of this county and pointed out some neighborhoods that could turn this election. No one looked up as I pointed toward where you could see a little bit of the General Electric plant that had once employed eighteen thousand people; just about everyone who lived here had an uncle, father, grandfather, sister, or mother who worked there. Today, after being known as GE Rail, it is called GE Transportation, owned by Wabtec, and only 2,200 people work there. Erie, like Vance's hometown of Middletown, is a region left behind by globalization, automation, and technology. The locomotive, tool and die shops, machine shops, and factories that once prospered here have struggled to rebuild and rebrand the region.

Erie is also the home of seventeen miles of pristine beaches along the Presque Isle peninsula. Blue-collar tourists from Ohio, Pennsylvania, western Maryland, and West Virginia flock here every summer to swim in Lake Erie, ride the waves, and stay in one of the hundreds of tourist cabins and campsites. It is also the home of a booming winery business.

After a while, I gave up trying to tell the reporters about this place. They didn't seem to notice that along the three-mile stretch the motorcade took to Gordon's, the streets in the neighborhoods and along US 19 were lined with Trump-Vance supporters. Some had stopped their cars to wave and get a glimpse of the Veep candidate; others had stepped out of their businesses or homes, and they were all waving. Several had Trump-Vance signs or American flags in their yards. One guy had a cheeky sign that read, "We Love Weird People."

I did not see a single reporter look up from their phone.

Inside Gordon's, Vance visited Firestone's Kitchen, where owner Kyle Bohrer gave him a tour even though the entire city block was without power. The place was packed with people wanting to take selfies, shake Vance's hand, or just say hello. Vance took the time to fulfill every request.

One of the cooks, Mark Spagel, gave the former marine a beer after everyone around the bar asked Vance to join the group in a toast.

After leaving Gordon's, we drove seven miles through neighborhoods and business districts to the airport, where Vance's campaign plane was waiting to take him to Wisconsin. The streets were packed with people cheering on the motorcade.

Something big was happening in Erie. Trump won this county in 2016—the first Republican to win it in decades. In 2020, he narrowly lost it to Biden. Both Fetterman and Shapiro won here in 2022. Mikus told me that Democrats would win Erie, but I was far from convinced.

Vance would go on to hold seventeen campaign rallies in Pennsylvania by Election Day. I attended most of them, interviewing him again in Johnstown, Butler, and Pittsburgh.

After the Pittsburgh interview in October, I told him I was finally interviewing his mom in Middletown, Ohio, the next day. He had my daughter Shannon snap a photo of us on his cell phone, and then he texted his mother to tell her that he was with me, joking, "Watch out."

Beverly Aikins is petite, with the same piercing blue eyes as her son, and proved to be as fun and bawdy as J. D. said she was. She is immensely proud of him and, most importantly, she embraces her role as a grandmother as fiercely as one would expect from a person who has been given a second chance.

On this day, that fierce love was accompanied by some pretty typical grandma shenanigans—Pokémon cards, to be exact—and parents who thought their children were being showered with too many of them by a certain grandma.

"Usha and J. D. have told me I cannot buy any more Pokémon cards.... I am cut off," she said with the kind of smile every grandmother has when the parents try to curtail a little spoiling.

Vance and his wife Usha told Aikins this at dinner the night before at a Skyline Chili restaurant where they had all gone for a family dinner. Aikins had the contraband cards ready to hand out to the kids, who were naturally unhappy with the turn of events.

Aikins said she leaned in and told them with a wink and a smile not to worry, that Grandma would work on their parents—something any grandparent does, including me.

"I see so much of J. D. in each of them," she said, laughing at her planned secret hijinks. "But it's a different kind of love. I can't even explain it, but they are—I would do absolutely anything for them." She spoke with the same awe you hear from grandparents across the world, describing the emotion that fills them when discussing their grandchildren.

She told me she has found redemption and peace through helping others who struggle with addiction. "It is a life of purpose."

In 2014, Aikins would not have been able to enjoy her relationship with her son, nor would she have been able to fulfill the other passion in her life—nursing—because of her debilitating addiction to alcohol, heroin, and pretty much anything else she used to get high. It had consumed every aspect of her life.

Beverly was the daughter of a turbulent marriage. Her mother, Bonnie Vance—"Mamaw" to J. D. Vance—was profoundly influential in her grandson's life and helped raise him with his older sister, Lindsay, when Beverly could not.

Vance recalled the ups and downs of his childhood with his mother's addiction in his 2016 memoir, which he wrote the year after she became sober.

Beverly made her debut on the national stage during the Republican National Convention when her son accepted former President Donald Trump's nomination to be his running mate.

The world saw the smiling Aikins, her thick, curly hair framing her face, glowing with pride and emotion as her son recalled the challenges in their lives before announcing that she had been sober for almost ten years—a proclamation that caused the crowd to rise onto their feet and burst into chants of "J. D.'s mom!"

Her addiction began with a powerful headache while working as a nurse at a hospital. She took a Vicodin pill and was astonished at how good she felt after taking it and the energy it gave her to do mundane household things, such as cleaning when she got home after a long day.

It was a high that led to wanting more, even at the cost of one of her biggest accomplishments, her nursing license.

As her addiction worsened, so did her temper and judgment. "I sold drugs from the hospital that I was working at—in particular, morphine. I stole morphine. I got caught. I got sent to treatment. And then I got out of treatment, and I was doing good for a while, and I relapsed. And I self-reported to the Ohio Board of Nursing that I had relapsed, and they suspended my license."

She was devastated, but not devastated enough to quit using, she said.

It was an eleven-year journey back that took her through addiction, poverty, shame, and sobriety to get her license back.

Vance told me in Pittsburgh, just before Beverly and I sat down to talk, that throughout his mother's journey and struggles in life, her compassion had remained intact—even when the drugs tried to rob it from her.

"I think Mom's always had a big heart," he said. "She's always loved people. She's always been one of those people who, you meet her and two minutes later you're, like, her best friend. And that's just a gift that she has.

"Obviously, she got sidetracked by the addiction issues. And it's a little bit of guesswork here, but I do think that one of the things—if you know somebody who's ever been addicted, they go through periods, maybe it's a few months, maybe it's a few years, where they're clean. And for me at least, I'd kind of given up hope that she would just be clean and stay clean."

Vance said he does not know what combination of the grace of God, faith, and purpose it was that got her to this moment of nearly ten years sober, "but it was some piece of all of that."

Their bond is formidable. He explained that while watching her make real progress in her recovery, as well as her dedication to getting her nursing license back and to being a good grandmother, it all finally came together for her, along with a little help from "honestly, the grace of God because, you can see, she wears this little cross necklace. And I think she has unconventional faith in a lot of ways, but it's still very real and very present. And that combination worked for her."

As for the drama around the Pokémon cards, Vance threw back his head and laughed. "She's a very good grandmother. She spoils them a little, you know what I mean?"

Of course, I do. I have four grandchildren. It is our inalienable right as grandmothers to do that.

By the time the debate between Vance and Walz took place, Vance had done scores of solo interviews. Walz had done one, with Harris, on CNN, and it went poorly. At the debate with Walz, Vance came across as polished; his critiques of Harris were sharp and to the point, but he was also polite and detailed on policy.

Walz struggled out of the gate, and once he did begin speaking, he never really engaged with Vance in a meaningful way.

Walz finally held his first solo interview in the first week of October, and by the end of the campaign, Vance had done a three-hour interview with podcaster Joe Rogan.

When I saw Vance at Trump's return trip to Butler in October, we were behind the stage in the click area surrounded by stacks of hay, with people hustling back and forth. The electricity of the event outside was palpable. The mood behind the scenes was emotional.

Vance told me privately how he felt to be there. "You know, I was supposed to be there that day," he said of July 13.

A staffer came to get me to do my interview with Trump, and the conversation ended. I never got to ask Vance for the rest of the story. Weeks later, he would tell Joe Rogan the rest of that story on air, how Trump toyed with having him come and announcing him as the pick in Butler.

"He [Trump] basically said, 'Well, I think I'm probably going to pick you, but I don't know, and I'm not ready to make a decision.' And then he looks at one of his staff members who's in the room. He's like, 'Actually, wouldn't it really set the world ablaze if we just made the decision today, and so why don't you come up with me and we'll just do the announcement in Butler, Pennsylvania?'"[18]

Ultimately, Vance told Rogan, Trump decided against his coming, saying that he still hadn't completely decided on him and the announcement needed to be better prepared.

As I listened to the Rogan podcast on my drive home from Trump's rally in Pittsburgh on election eve, I thought about the gravity of that decision. Thomas Crooks could have picked off both men on that stage, just like that French Indian scout could have picked off George Washington 250 years earlier. Was it just luck? Was it simply Washington moving ever so slightly to the left? Was it just happenstance that Trump hadn't yet made up his mind about Vance?

I went back to my notes of my conversation with Trump on July 14: "It was an act of God, Salena," he'd said. "It was the hand of God. He was there."

Indeed. For all three men.

Chapter 9

There Is No There There ...

PITTSBURGH, Pennsylvania

On August 13, a Democratic source contacted several local and national press outlets with the news that Vice President Kamala Harris and her running mate, Minnesota governor Tim Walz, would travel to the Democratic National Convention in Chicago by bus, and the tour would kick off in Pittsburgh.

The Walz rollout had been bumpy. A central theme emerged: He makes stuff up—from exaggerating his role in handling "weapons of war" in the military as a reservist, to how many times he visited China, to his repeated claim that he was in Hong Kong when China's communist rulers crushed prodemocracy protests in Tiananmen Square. He also had to walk back his claim that he and his wife used IVF, a fertility treatment that became politically charged, and his claim that he had received an award from the Nebraska Chamber of Commerce for his work in the business community.

Those stories, however, were mostly shared by center-right news organizations and hadn't seen much daylight in the mainstream media.

It was a big deal that Harris and Walz would kick off their tour in Pittsburgh. It showed they knew they had to win Pennsylvania to win the White House. I picked up the phone and started calling all the Democrat operatives I had known for decades to find out where the rally would be held. My first call was to Rich Fitzgerald, the former county executive who had retired months earlier after being term-limited from running again.

"I haven't heard a thing," Fitzgerald said. *That's odd. Fitz knows everything*, I thought.

I called Mike Mikus, who was running Malcolm Kenyatta's statewide race for auditor general. Surely, he would know because I knew his candidate would be hamming it up on the stage with them; there's not a stage or a camera that Kenyatta can pass by.

"I have no idea," Mikus said.

I found nothing on social media either, other than a few local folks complaining that they didn't know where it was going to be held, and they wanted to attend. The night before, a Democrat with ties to labor told me there were buses lined up at the union hall to take union members and committee members to Harris's Pittsburgh rally. The only problem was that the rally wasn't being held in Pittsburgh; it was to be in the parking lot at Pittsburgh International Airport.

The kicker was that the event was invite-only, mostly union members of the Service Employees International Union (SEIU), which is more of a social justice union than a labor union. Why weren't they letting the public know where the rally would be? Why was this event invite-only? No one could provide an answer.

I called Josh Shapiro, but he didn't answer his phone.

By the morning of the event, the national news organizations were still billing it as a "big kickoff bus tour" from Pittsburgh to the Democratic National Convention in Chicago, with a stop in all-important Erie.[1] After exhaustive calls and texts, I found out the rally was now to be held at a private airport hangar seventeen miles from the city limits and would be attended only by invited members of the SEIU and some Democratic Committee people.

The "rally" was tiny. Harris was with her husband, Second Gentleman Doug Emhoff, and Walz. After the short event, they headed to a local Democratic Party headquarters in Rochester, Beaver County. Few if any in Beaver County knew Harris was coming, so no one was there to greet her if they wanted to show support.

Beaver County is located west of Allegheny County, adjacent to Pittsburgh International Airport. Once upon a time, not too long ago, the county was a potent component of the Democratic Party, filled with union families who worked at steel mills in Aliquippa and Ambridge.

But as the Democratic Party shifted leftward, many voters moved toward the Republican Party. In 2020, then-President Donald Trump won the county over Joe Biden by nearly twenty percentage points.

Several longtime Democratic strategists in Pennsylvania believed that Harris skipped Pittsburgh so she could avoid the possibility of protesters interrupting her tour in the important battleground state.

Meanwhile, on X, many of Harris's potential supporters expressed disappointment in not being able to see her when she was in Beaver County.

The details of the event were kept quiet until Harris's arrival. Given the distance between Beaver County and the city of Pittsburgh, it was difficult for her many city supporters to get there in time to see her, and it was obvious that voters wanted to see her in person. However, for whatever reason, this campaign chose to tightly control the event and allow only the people they wanted to attend.

The bus tour was hardly a bus tour—it did a thirty-four-mile loop with stops that included Primanti Bros. restaurant, known for its signature sandwiches topped with coleslaw and french fries. After regular patrons were cleared out, thirty invited guests, mostly Democratic Committee members who were told to arrive early and park several parking lots away, were seated in booths and ready to greet Harris and Walz.[2]

Harris finished the day's visit at a Sheetz gas station, which seemed ironic at the very least and hypocritical at the most, considering that the Biden-Harris administration had sued Sheetz in April, less than a day after President Biden visited there. The ludicrous lawsuit claimed that by conducting criminal background checks on job applicants, the company was practicing racial discrimination.

As I watched these two stops play out in western Pennsylvania, I was astonished at how particularly tone-deaf Harris's campaign was—both Sheetz and Primanti Bros. are locally owned icons in this region, so you shouldn't kick customers out of the latter and pretend you are not suing the former and think it is great optics to showcase that.

Sheetz employs nearly twenty-five thousand people along a stretch of Appalachia that cuts diagonally through most of Pennsylvania and parts of West Virginia, Virginia, Maryland, Ohio, and North Carolina. The company gives back to its communities through a charitable foundation and has a tradition on the Fourth of July of honoring customers by rolling back prices on all types of fuel except diesel at all 675-plus locations. That day's fuel cost is always $1.76 per gallon, a tribute to the founding year of 1776.

In Pennsylvania, going after Sheetz is like tugging on Superman's cape, especially in central and western Pennsylvania, where pulling up to a Sheetz station is like pulling up to home. The alleged violation was particularly egregious, as it described a common-sense practice, a good business practice. Any company would want to make sure its employees who interact with the public aren't criminals.

Harris's stops at both places told locals two things: she wanted to use them for their value as a sense of place by staging vanity stops, but she was hoping people weren't paying attention to any messy associations involving the businesses.

Harris and Walz never made it to Erie on that bus, and they didn't ride the bus to Chicago, either—they headed back to the airport for a forty-five-minute flight to Chicago, never once attempting to earn a new voter. To the casual observer, however, the event probably looked picture-perfect.

National news organizations with no ties to Pennsylvania culture wrote dreamy stories about Harris's whimsical "small-town" bus trip across western Pennsylvania.[3] Most of these reports touted that Harris was now leading Donald Trump in Pennsylvania, after a *New York Times*/Siena College poll released days before showed Harris with a slight edge over Trump among Pennsylvania voters, a margin of 45 percent to 43 percent.[4]

I called a very plugged-in Democratic operative in Pittsburgh's Squirrel Hill neighborhood and deconstructed all the details of the day.

"Am I crazy? I feel like I am," I said. "They did nothing to win over new voters. They took zero risks and even put themselves in places that could have backlash."

He had two thoughts: first, maybe they were trying to keep things tight so no pro-Palestine protesters would ruin their events, and second, he repeated the Gertrude Stein quote mentioned by several other Democrats of the campaign's decisions: "Maybe there is no *there* there."

———

For the next week, the media hailed the Democratic National Convention as an instrument of joy, framing it as a way to move past Trump's dominance in American culture.

Dane Strother, a legendary Democratic strategist who was in Chicago, called to tell me the enthusiasm around the convention hall was off the wall.

The day after the convention ended, Trump announced at a campaign rally in Arizona, with Robert F. Kennedy Jr. at his side, that the former Democrat was endorsing him.

The *New York Times* reported that Kennedy's endorsement would likely have no impact on the race; Kennedy had little support in the polls as an independent candidate.[5] But the paper missed that Kennedy represented the part of the coalition that Trump was building that was part populist, part conservative, and part disruptive.

In particular, working-class and college-educated suburban moms who were unhappy with the additives in the foods their children ate and the impact that school shutdowns during the pandemic had on their families liked what Kennedy was saying about those issues.

The *New York Times* pegged Kennedy as a bearer of grievances, similar to how the paper pegged Trump, but many voters in Pennsylvania found that having Kennedy on board made them like Trump more.[6]

The *Times* also got the grievance thing wrong. This cycle was very different. This cycle was very aspirational; people really felt like they were part of something much bigger than 2016.

Trump pollster Tony Fabrizio put out a memo saying, "This is good news for President Trump and his campaign—plain and simple," writing that a majority of Kennedy voters already broke overwhelmingly in Trump's favor.[7]

The Kennedy announcement took some of the wind out of Harris's sails in Pennsylvania. By Tuesday, August 27, she announced that she would do her first sit-down news interview with Dana Bash at CNN. Walz would join her. It would be her first interview with the press since she became the Democratic nominee forty days earlier.

There is no better summation of the August 29 interview than the one *New York Times* columnist Bret Stephens penned immediately afterward:

> She [Harris] was vague to the point of vacuous. She struggled to give straight answers to her shifting positions on fracking and border security other than to say, "My values have not changed." Fine, but she evaded the question of why it took the Biden administration more than three years to gain better control of the border, which it ultimately did through an executive order that could have been in place years earlier. It also didn't answer the question of why she reversed her former policy positions—or whether she has higher values other than political expediency.
>
> Harris also relied on a few talking points that may not serve her well in the next two months. She mentioned price gouging, but Americans probably won't believe that grocery chains with razor-thin profit margins are the real culprits when it comes to their rising food bills. Her $100 billion plan to give first-time home buyers $25,000 in down payment support would mainly be an incentive for ever-higher

home prices. Even Trump may be smart enough to explain just how inflationary the gimmick could be.

A bigger weakness in the interview was the presence of Harris's running mate, Governor Tim Walz of Minnesota. Though he delivered a fine speech at the Democratic National Convention (brightly enhanced by his cheering son, Gus), he was transparently evasive in answering Bash's questions about his misstatement about his military service, false claims about a DUI arrest and misleading statements about his family's fertility treatments. If there are other lies or untruths in Walz's record, the campaign ought to get ahead of them now.[8]

One day later, the White House announced that President Biden and Vice President Harris would join in with events surrounding Pittsburgh's iconic Labor Day parade. It is the largest parade in the country, in terms of the number of union participants.[9]

Union organizers estimate that Biden has marched in this parade two dozen times over the past forty years. His most memorable march happened in 2015, when he trotted through the mile-long parade route, slapping backs, giving hugs, shaking hands, and stopping to talk to the union families who were lined up to see him. He was then vice president and had not yet decided to seek the presidency. Already, former Secretary of State Hillary Clinton was in the primary race, flush with money and ahead in the polls, and so was Senator Bernie Sanders, a Vermont independent.

Wearing a white polo shirt and beaming with fitness and energy, Biden skipped through the streets, leaving reporters and Secret Service agents in his wake. He was met with cheers of "Run, Joe, run!" I honestly had never seen anything like it before. When a gaggle of reporters asked whether he was going to run, Biden, then seventy-two, quipped, "I am going to run part of the parade."[10]

A month later, Biden announced that he had simply "run out of time" to mount a real presidential campaign.[11]

This time, a very different Biden was coming back for the Labor Day Parade. His gait was slow, his movements painfully stiff. Gone were the one-offs and back-slapping; he was now within months of leaving office, after being forced out of running for a second term, and his vice president, Kamala Harris, would be the real draw. The rank-and-file union voters in western Pennsylvania were the ones who narrowly placed Biden over Trump in 2020—he likely felt an obligation to rally them for Harris to preserve his legacy.

Harris has never had to win over a blue-collar voter to win an election in her home state of California. As a consequence, she struggled to express her stand on the issue of fossil fuels, fracking, and regulations that hamper the vitality of the manufacturing sector in the state. According to the Bureau of Labor Statistics, Pennsylvania is home to 749,000 union members.[12] Harris needed their votes. She needed to be seen with these voters. So, they were coming back to Pittsburgh.

Again, no advance information was given about when Biden and Harris would join the parade. When I called local party and Democratic sources whom I have relied on for years, I was met with "I have no idea."

I called Justin Merriman, a photojournalist who works for the *Washington Post* locally, to ask if he knew anything about the parade. He had no idea, and he wanted to cover the event, he told me in frustration.

With only hours to spare, Manuel Bonder, as good a staffer for Shapiro as Luke Schroeder is for J. D. Vance, told me Biden and Harris would appear at the International Brotherhood of Electrical Workers union hall on Pittsburgh's South Side in the late afternoon. And no, neither Biden nor Harris would walk in the parade. The public was not told where they would be. Once again, any chance for a curious voter or supporter to show up and see Harris was squelched.

Standing outside the union hall, I saw there were no supporters to greet Biden and Harris. I guessed they really didn't know they were in there. *Geez*, I thought, watching as union members who were attending filed inside. I saw three guys I knew whom I knew to be Trump supporters. *My goodness, it is all over their Facebook pages*, I thought.

I was later told that union leadership leaned on members to attend the event.

I found the situation bewildering. In all the years I've covered Democratic politics in western Pennsylvania, a place dominated by Democratic control, I'd never seen anything like this campaign. My union member friend agreed.

Inside the hall were about thirty-five round tables, each seating ten people, mostly men. I saw more people I recognized as people whom I had thought were Trump supporters from past interactions. There really was no *there* there to this campaign. It was all smoke and mirrors.

But why? Merriman and I, who have covered politics together for decades, went back and forth over the phone the next day. We decided there was no need for the smoke and mirrors. Harris should be able to draw a crowd. Didn't her campaign want to assess the enthusiasm of supporters? I mentioned that they might have been afraid of encountering "Free Palestine" protesters, and Merriman agreed it was a possibility. Pittsburgh's elected offices have been taken over by the Democratic Socialists of America, and there is certainly a strong strain of antisemitism in the local party ranks. *Or were they simply that bad at this?*[13]

President Biden walked out onto the stage to chants of "Thank you, Joe!" His speech lasted twenty minutes, and he concluded by telling the union members he will soon be "on the sidelines," but he added, "Are you ready to elect Kamala Harris as the next president of the United States of America?"[14]

Harris took to the stage and said little other than announcing that she joined Biden's opposition to the sale of Pittsburgh-based US Steel to Japanese firm Nippon Steel Corporation. She did not mention fracking for natural gas, a major industry in Pennsylvania that almost everyone in that hall was working in and or around, and one that she had once forcefully argued would end if she became president.

Harris and Biden left. But less than thirty-six hours later, the White House announced that Harris would spend September 5 to 10—almost a full week—in Pittsburgh to prepare for the presidential debate in Philadelphia the following week. Walz would also be in Pittsburgh on September 4 and 5. Yet if any details were released about planned public appearances for either candidate during their stay, I never found them. Neither did Merriman.

Democrats hold a massive voter registration lead in Pittsburgh, where a Republican hasn't won anything since a majority on the county commission in the mid-1990s, followed by a Republican county executive and a mayor's race nearly one hundred years earlier, before the onset of the Great Depression when former President Franklin D. Roosevelt created the New Deal Democratic coalition. So, the optics made sense.

After numerous calls to county Democratic Party chairs, I found out that Walz would begin his swing through Pennsylvania on September 4 with visits to Lancaster and Erie counties. There was confusion about whether he would be in Pittsburgh.

He started his trip to Pennsylvania the day before Harris arrived by visiting the Lancaster County Democratic Committee field office with his daughter Hope. Reporter Alyssa Kratz noted that he spoke for six to seven minutes and would not take questions from the Lancaster media. Nor, Kratz said, were local pool reporters allowed to put up microphones anywhere near Walz.[15]

When one local reporter shouted out a question, a Walz campaign staffer scolded the reporters in attendance, telling them to "not disrupt the program."[16]

It is important to note that the program was over when that happened and Walz had finished talking with volunteers. So, there was literally nothing to interrupt.

Walz stopped at the Cherry Hill Orchards in New Danville, where he also chose not to answer questions from the press—but he did get a gob, the Pennsylvania Dutch version of an oversized Oreo cookie.

After his brief visit to Lancaster County, Walz flew to Pittsburgh, where he got a mint chocolate chip milkshake with his daughter at a Moon Township creamery right by the airport, and then he drove one hour and forty minutes to a Fayette County farm.

There were no gaggles for the press at the first stop or the dairy farm stop located in ruby-red Fayette County, where Trump-Vance signs adorned almost every other home.

Walz ate cheese curds. The farm owners told Walz they support solar energy but not on productive farmland and that natural gas should be a resource that is tapped, not spurned.

It was awkward; both positions ran counter to the preferences of many in the Democratic Party. It made me wonder who had done the advance work for this visit. Farmers in Pennsylvania often receive generous royalties from natural gas wells on their property. In fact, more than $193 million in royalties have gone toward subsidizing family farmers by helping them buy equipment, hire workers, or pay down debt.

In 2024, the Biden-Harris administration placed a pause on liquefied natural gas (LNG) exports that come from farms like the one Walz was visiting, hurting their bottom lines.

A statewide Pennsylvania poll conducted on the issue showed a whopping 58 percent of Pennsylvania voters opposed the Biden-Harris LNG export moratorium. The poll also found that 41 percent of voters were more likely to vote against Biden based on his suspending approvals for new facilities that export LNG, with only 22 percent of voters more likely to support him.[17]

Just a few days before Walz's visit, during the CNN interview, Harris said of fracking that her climate change values hadn't changed, and Walz nodded vigorously in agreement.

Now Walz returned to Pittsburgh to prepare for his rally at Highmark Amphitheater in Erie, but not before ghosting his press pool in the morning and eating breakfast at a local diner. (The diner was favored so much by President Barack Obama in 2008 that it served pancakes during his inaugural celebrations.)

Pool reporter Aaron Pellish of CNN noted on X that he had to rely on a staffer at the restaurant for details about Walz's visit because, of course, the campaign was stiffing the media.[18]

There was a clear pattern developing. Both Harris's and Walz's visits to western Pennsylvania in the past few weeks had been tightly controlled events, often invite-only, and they were custom-made to come across as authentic, flawless, and generating enthusiasm among the voters.

There had been no meaningful interaction with the local press. Heck, there had been no meaningful interaction with curious voters or supporters. Few national reporters seemed to grasp this, and that was an important flaw in the campaign: either Harris had no enthusiastic supporters or her staffers were really, really bad at running campaigns.

Everyone is missing how big they are blowing this, I thought.

But most of the press, nationally and locally, kept running stories about things voters cared little about, while missing what was happening right under their noses.

To again quote iconic nineteenth-century American novelist Gertrude Stein—who, by the way, was from Pittsburgh and originated the line—truly, there was no *there* there.

The constant refusal by Harris and Walz to discuss matters such as crime, homelessness, or the effect of inflation on Pennsylvanians' budgets was profoundly important—and the most important interaction a candidate can have is with a local reporter. Those journalists often are lifelong residents or have called the region they cover home for a long time. They understand the challenges in the community and know that their readers or viewers want to know how candidates would address them.

A longtime Pennsylvania Democrat finally admitted to me what he thought was going on: "The plan is to run out the clock with tightly orchestrated events to avoid little to any contact with the press. They see this tactic as having little risk. They are banking that voters don't want more from their presidential candidates."

Walz headed to Erie. Again, the event was invite-only. But the venue was large, so local Pittsburgh Democrats were soon besieged with pleas to travel the two hours to Erie. When I arrived, there were scores of buses lined up a few blocks away.

Harris had been in Pittsburgh for over two days. She was holed up in the historic Omni William Penn Hotel in Downtown, which has welcomed every sitting president since Theodore Roosevelt to its presidential suite.

She made one appearance during the entire debate-prep stay in Pittsburgh—and it was a doozy. She correctly decided to visit

Pittsburgh's Strip District, a famed neighborhood filled with fourth- and fifth-generation epicurean shops, ethnic grocery stores, and restaurants as well as a chocolatier, a fish market, and even a whiskey distillery. It's one of the city's fastest-growing neighborhoods, with expensive loft apartments and condominiums. Everyone flocks there, whether a local or a tourist.

However, this was the last correct decision she made. Among the more than one hundred small businesses there—places with a cultural connection for almost anyone who has grown up in or visited western Pennsylvania—her advance team picked the only business along Penn Avenue that is a franchise: Penzeys Spices.

This, after spending countless days in the city researching the Strip businesses and thoroughly checking business owners' backgrounds, including their worldviews and social media posts; this pick was not decided in a vacuum.

Any halfway decent advance team knows exactly where it's placing its boss. Anyone with a rudimentary ability to use Google can type in "best places to go in Pittsburgh's Strip District" and find Pennsylvania Macaroni, Wigle Whiskey, and the Senator John Heinz History Center.

What never comes up in such a Google search is Penzeys Spices. In fact, a simple Google search of Penzeys Spices would reveal several key points pretty quickly. The owner is a Democrat, which is fine and safe for this candidate. But read further, and things go south fast in terms of comportment—something Harris, many Democrats, and almost every member of the media enjoy criticizing about Trump.

The owner of Penzeys Spices is really, well, *out there*, which is not new information.

In two successive emails to his customers in 2022, he sent out a "Republicans Are Racist" weekend special for Martin Luther King Jr. Day.

And for those not on the Penzeys Spices email list, he posted the message on the company's website to ensure that everyone saw it. Days later, he ran another "All Republicans Are Racists" special that begged the remaining loyal Penzeys Spices customers—the owner acknowledged in a Facebook post that the store had lost forty thousand of them—to buy gift cards.[19]

When a candidate visits a city, they typically go to a locally owned place, which often has nostalgic emotions attached to it and is a cultural touchstone that draws people together, such as Pennsylvania Macaroni, which has been in the Sunseri family for several generations. The shop is a quintessential establishment for everyone from the area, no matter what their politics are. It sells just as many spices as Penzeys and is right across the street.

Nonetheless, Harris walked into Penzeys, was greeted by a weeping elderly supporter, and then said, "It is time to turn the page on the divisiveness. It's time to bring our country together, chart a new way forward."[20]

Harris had a say in where she went in Pittsburgh. Her advance team had every reason to know full well that Penzeys was not a place where anyone would turn the page on divisiveness. This was a place where divisiveness is part of who they are. By going to Penzeys Spices, Harris showed every reporter who she is. And yet few in the press pool that day told the whole story.

Instead, a *Washington Post* report posted on X noted, "Kamala just went into Penzeys Spices and bought Creamy Peppercorn Dressing Base, Fox Point Seasoning, Trinidad Lemon-Garlic Marinade, Turkish Seasoning, and Tuscan Sunset Salt Free Italian Seasoning."[21]

An Associated Press headline read, "Harris turns to her favorite foods in effort to show a more private side and connect with voters." The story then went on about collard greens in a tub, caramel cake, pancakes, bacon breakfasts, and how much of a devoted foodie Harris is.[22]

MSNBC ran a breaking news headline across the screen that read: NOW: HARRIS VISITS SMALL BUSINESS IN PITTS-BURGH, with her hugging a crying supporter.[23]

But there were few in the moment who questioned her about the divisiveness of her choices.

Harris wasn't trying to highlight her devotion to food by visiting Penzeys Spices. Rather, by doing so, she showed people and the press who she is without answering a single question about her choices, and no one questioned it, likely because they share her values and see nothing divisive about going to a place that makes their biases against Republicans part of their business model.

Except no one in the national press had spent a minute doing research on the place, or, if they did, they saw no problem with this perspective.

The next day, September 8, Harris and her husband were seen for the last time during her debate-prep time in Pittsburgh, and it was only from a distance as they took a walk along the grounds of the military base next to Pittsburgh International Airport. She gave pool reporters a thumbs-up when someone shouted, "Are you ready for the debate?"

Harris left Pittsburgh the next day for the debate at Philadelphia's National Constitution Center.

I opted out of covering the debate at the event center. Journalists are placed in a room somewhat adjacent to the debate floor where reporters echo their perceptions of the debate among each other. That's fine, but journalists are not going to decide the election—voters in my backyard are.

So, I went to a bar to watch the debate, sat back, and observed people's reactions. The first time I did this was in 2016 when

Merriman and I went to the Tin Lizzy in Youngstown, Pennsylvania, a bar over a hundred years old, where patrons were young to middle-aged and almost all Democrats. We watched the first debate between Trump and Hillary Clinton, and it was eye-popping to listen to these Democrats who pointed to Trump as the winner. Almost all of them told me afterward that they were going to vote for him.

This time, I settled in at a local bar and watched people watch the debate. Hands down, they thought on merit that Harris won. But it also didn't matter—their votes had not changed. If they went in voting for her, they were still intending to vote for her. If they went in voting for Trump, most of them were still voting for him.

All the news stories the next day said Harris won the debate—and she had. I went on Fox News the next morning with Dana Perino and Bill Hemmer to offer my assessment: "The debate changed nothing."

I understood that, and the following weeks of reporting proved it. Harris won, but it didn't matter because Trump was still ahead in polls, and it was hard to imagine him losing this race in my home state.

It wasn't until December 2024 that I understood how spot-on my reporting was when I called Trump's pollster Tony Fabrizio, who had been around for all three races, and he told me I had been dead right.

"Trump lost no ground—none," he said of the first post-debate poll, which he admitted pretty much shocked him.

Chris LaCivita told me that same month, "It was the craziest thing I'd ever seen," adding that he wondered at the time if I had talked to Fabrizio because I had nailed exactly what the polls showed them.

And it was all on the backs of the conservative populist coalition I had written about with Brad Todd in 2017, a coalition that had expanded among the working class. The Democrats and the press had a blind spot; they siloed the working class by race, except that was not how the working class was voting—working-class whites were voting side by side with working-class Black and Hispanic people.

They all shared the same connective tissue and that was "place." They lived by each other, many of them for generations, they worked beside each other, they went to church together, they coached each other's kids in Little League and soccer. I wrote many stories in Philadelphia and Pittsburgh about how the Black middle-class and working-class voters were moving to the right. These reports were often ignored.

I went on Fox News a couple of days after the debate and was asked how the race looked. I broke it down this way: "We will wake up the day after the election and find out that it was a cosmetologist, welder, waitress, and machinist who has decided this election. They are going to be younger and more diverse than you understand, and they are moving towards Trump."

After her debate prep, Harris would make two more trips to Pittsburgh before Election Day—in between, President Barack Obama would pinch hit for her as well.

She gave an economic policy speech at Carnegie Mellon University for the Economic Club on September 25—and yes, it was invite-only, so all that opportunity to have young people attend was quashed. At that point, I gave up trying to figure out her campaign.

Obama's visit to Pittsburgh was something else. The former president was returning to a very different western Pennsylvania from the one he had won robustly in 2008 and less so in 2012.

In 2008, Obama ran on a message of aspiration, using the slogan of "Hope and Change" to create a coalition of working-class white people long part of the New Deal Democrats, minorities, young people, and educated professionals.

In that race, against Republican John McCain, he won eighteen of Pennsylvania's sixty-seven counties. Here in the west, he won Cambria and Erie and came within one hundred votes in Fayette, and he earned a whopping 57 percent in Allegheny County. Overall, in Pennsylvania, Obama earned 3,276,363 raw votes, or 54.47 percent, compared to McCain's 2,655,885, or 44.15 percent.

By the time he ran in 2012, Obama's hope and change were gone, replaced by a more ideological Democratic Party built around climate change, expansive government, internationalism, and a move toward eliminating fossil fuels.

His new coalition of ascendant demographics—minorities, young people, college-educated white elites, and women—was his focus. Left in the dust were New Deal Democrats. But it worked. Just enough New Deal Democrats stayed with him. However, his slippage in support should have been a warning sign to Democrats that this dismissal of working-class interests might not work for the next Democratic candidate.

When Obama won Pennsylvania and the presidency in 2012, he did so by being the first president in modern political history to win his second term with fewer voters than in his first run for president.

That was no more evident than in western Pennsylvania, where the erosion of support was noticeable if you were paying attention. Obama lost five counties that year, slipping to a narrow thirteen of sixty-seven. He lost a percentage point in Allegheny County, lost Cambria County, lost Fayette County significantly, and counties like Beaver, where the race had been much closer in 2008, shifted right.

In Pennsylvania in 2012, Obama earned 2,990,274 votes, or just over 51 percent, meaning nearly three hundred thousand people who voted for him before just didn't show up. Now, the interesting thing about that is those missing voters did not show up for GOP candidate Mitt Romney, who won just 2,680,434, or 46 percent, of the vote.

In short, Romney gained just over 24,000 voters over McCain in Pennsylvania that year, while Obama lost nearly 300,000 state-wide, with many of those voters coming from western Pennsylvania. Obama lost around 20,000 voters in Allegheny County, a county he won, but the diminishing support in Beaver was around 3,000 votes; Westmoreland, 8,000 votes; Fayette, 4,000 votes; Cambria, 8,000 votes; and Butler County, around 4,000 votes.

So, where did the former Obama voters go if they didn't go to Romney? For the most part, it appears they stayed home. They liked the promise of Obama in 2008 and generally liked him personally, but later, they did not like his policies, and they saw Romney not as the guy who would bring jobs back but as the guy who would come to your desk with a box to escort you out of the building after he politely fired you.

The Obama "Coalition of the Ascendant" promised to pay dividends for his party for years to come. For former Secretary of State Hillary Clinton, that was not the case. She lost a state that her husband, President Bill Clinton, had won. Then-candidate Joe Biden, because of his past relationships with unions, was able to glue on just enough of the working-class vote in 2020 to win the state narrowly.

That working-class vote—white, Black, Hispanic, and Asian— was now decidedly in the Republican camp. The party had become the party of work. A part of the coalition that was always delegated to the sidelines was now in the driver's seat.

And Obama apparently knew that.

Before his event at the University of Pittsburgh, Obama visited a Democratic field office in East Liberty and vented hard at Black voters, particularly men.

He walked in and said to the press pool that he needed to "speak some truths," particularly with Black men because he was hearing that "we have not yet seen the same kinds of energy and turnout in all quarters of our neighborhoods and communities as we saw when I was running."[24]

He continued:

Now, I also want to say that that seems to be more pronounced with the brothers. When you have a choice that is this clear. When, on the one hand, you have somebody who grew up like you, knows you, went to college with you, understands the struggles and pain and joy that comes from those experiences, who's had to work harder and do more and overcome and achieves the second highest office in the land, and is putting forward concrete proposals to directly address the things that are vital in our neighborhoods and our communities.

And that's all one side. And on the other side, you have someone who has consistently shown disregard, not just for the communities, but for you as a person, and you're thinking about sitting out? And you're coming up with all kinds of reasons and excuses? I've got a problem with that because— because part of it makes me think, and I'm speaking to men directly now, part of it makes me think that, well, you just aren't feeling the idea of having a woman as president, and you're coming up with other alternatives and other reasons for that.

They've been raising us and working and having our backs, and when we get in trouble and the system's not working for us, they're the ones who are out there marching and protesting and—and so now you're thinking about sitting out or even supporting somebody who has a history of denigrating you because you think that's a sign of strength? Because that's what being a man is, putting women down? That's not acceptable.

He would go on to land a divisive rally later at the University of Pittsburgh, but the mask was off. Black men were not doing what he wanted them to do. The Black men and women I interviewed in Pittsburgh and Philadelphia found it insulting to be lectured by him, even more so after he then went out to speak to an all-white audience.

Rico Elmore, who voted for Obama twice and is Black, told me bluntly, "This is why I left the party. Don't come here and lecture me about who you think I should vote for because of my race."

Harris returned to Pittsburgh on Election Night—for a total of nine minutes. This time, however, there was no invite needed for her election eve event. It was a star-studded concert with singer and actress Andra Day, actor and comedian Cedric the Entertainer, and pop singer Katy Perry. The party, held at the Carrie Blast Furnaces National Historic Landmark, was filled with mostly white, middle-aged women.

Harris was about to find out if waiting for the clock to run out was a good plan.

Chapter 10

"As I Was Saying . . ."

BUTLER, *Pennsylvania*

My alarm went off at 3:30 a.m., and I jumped out of bed immediately.

The truth is, I hadn't slept much at all that night. I got up at 12:03 a.m., 1:30 a.m., and 2:10 a.m., each time with my heart racing, and I frantically checked my clock to make sure I hadn't somehow missed the alarm and would be late getting to the Butler Farm Show Complex.

It was October 5, 2024, less than three months after President Donald Trump had been shot there, a shooting that took the life of firefighter Corey Comperatore and injured two other attendees, and Trump was heading back to the site for another rally.

He asked me in Harrisburg at the end of July what I thought about his going back, and I told him it would be good for him personally so that no lingering fears remained attached to that place. He had nodded in agreement, and then said, "What about the people of Butler? Would it be good for them? They are my people; they are always there for me."

"It would be very good for the people of Butler. They need this more than you do."

The rally wouldn't start for fifteen more hours, but I wanted to get there to do a couple of *Fox & Friends* segments at the site by 5:30 a.m. And I needed to look halfway decent—not my clothes, but my *hair*. I'm Italian, with untamable curly Italian hair inherited from my parents. Even though it was October, the forecast was for a hot and humid day, with temperatures over 80 degrees Fahrenheit. That meant spending a good hour straightening my hair if it was going to be halfway decent-looking for television and at least thirteen hours in the sun.

This wasn't the first time I'd been back to the site. I went there previously to walk the grounds and retrace my movements on July 13.

That first time I went back after the shooting, it felt surreal. Also, isolating. I went alone, and there was no one to walk the grounds with me who had shared my experience.

This time, I got within five miles of the rally site and, even though it was still dark outside, the roads along the way were lit up with Trump flags, Trump signs, Trump voters, and vendor stands. People were waving at the passersby. Some had set up tailgating, and some had festooned their trucks and cars with decorations. *Oh boy, this looks big*, I thought. Within two miles of the farm show grounds entrance, I encountered a string of brake lights. *I'm going to be late for my hit.* I called the producer, who told me not to worry; they'd push me back to 7:00 a.m.

I decided to opt out of the press parking area, which is separate from where the rally-goers park, because I really wanted to immerse myself in the moment. It was barely 6:00 a.m. and the parking lot was nearly full, with a line to get in that stretched for a good mile. Despite that, it looked like the place was already packed with people.

It was hard to deny the energy—joy, aspiration, and feeling part of something bigger than oneself. It was palpable. Yes, something big was happening here. I had seen evidence that this support was building just a little over a week before when Trump went to Indiana, Pennsylvania, for a rally.

He had started that day early in the tiny town of Smithton, on a farm surrounded by cornfields and rolling hills, for a policy roundtable in a barn with local farmers. Trump had listened intently as third-, fourth-, and fifth-generation farmers shared stories about their struggles to maintain their calling of providing the country with a food supply.

Smithton was known for two things in its long history: It was the home of Stoney's beer and the home of actress and singer Shirley Jones, whose parents had owned the massive brewery.

The farmers told Trump that many of them keep the family farms going because of the royalties from the natural gas extracted from their land. They were worried about the Biden-Harris administration's moratorium on exporting liquefied natural gas. They told Trump in no uncertain terms that this would have a devastating impact on their livelihoods.

From there, Trump got in his motorcade, as did my daughter Shannon and I, who were there to interview him. He did something for the next few hours that I had not seen a presidential candidate do in ages: he rode through two expansive counties, taking the backroads, passing through small towns with schools, churches, tiny business districts, and rural farmland. Everywhere his motorcade went, the streets were filled with well-wishers waving their hands, their flags, and their shirts in support of him.

One family was sitting on a tractor. As we passed over the Pennsylvania Turnpike, we saw people waving from on top of several tractor-trailers in stopped traffic.

Shannon, sitting with me and Justin Wells, who was producing a documentary on Trump for the Tucker Carlson Network, was peering out of the motorcade's window in amazement.

We made our way to the postindustrial borough of Kittanning in Armstrong County where we stopped at a tiny family grocery called Sprankle's Neighborhood Market. Inside, Trump made his way around the modest store, talking to the employees. He bought some Utz pretzels. With him were Suzie Wiles and Chris LaCivita, and he intentionally mentioned them by name. This was not for the people in the store but for the media who continued to pen vicious stories that he would soon be firing both of his aides. He knew what he was doing; Trump rewards loyalty. I was hidden at the back of a pack of reporters, hard to see because I'm not that tall. A lot of the reporters were with local news outlets, and I wanted them to have a chance to ask him questions. I knew I'd have that opportunity later, so I held back.

But Trump spotted me.

"Salena! There is my Salena," he said. My daughter elbowed me, laughing at my awkward discomfort at the attention. He spied Shannon and said her name over and over again. Her face turned red. I was enjoying it.

When Trump went to pay for his Utz pretzels, he saw Jennifer Krantz in the checkout line with her boys, Brayden, Eddie, and Frederick, and her husband Bryant. He reached into his pocket, grabbed what looked like a money clip, and handed the clerk a $100 bill.

"Here, it is going to go down a little bit," Trump told the clerk, to everyone's astonishment.

"Thank you so much," Jennifer said, a little stunned by the help. As Trump left, I asked her what that meant to her, and she said, "Having three growing boys means buying a lot of groceries and that has put a big strain on our budget. It has been very difficult."

We headed to Indiana, Pennsylvania. All in all, that day—just days after another apparent attempt on Trump's life, this time at a golf course, which Secret Service agents thwarted before any shots were fired—we traversed more than one hundred miles through Allegheny, Armstrong, Indiana, and Westmoreland Counties. Trump saw firsthand how things were in small towns, and he was greeted spontaneously by thousands of people.

It was a striking contrast to the three-stop tour that Harris did at Pittsburgh International Airport.

Butler was a greater continuum of the enthusiasm and energy. After talking to hundreds of supporters in line, I made my way to the press entrance. There I saw Michel Picard for the first time since the shooting. We locked eyes, and a wave of emotion overcame both of us. We ran toward each other and hugged.

Picard wasn't dressed in his usual dapper suit and Ray-Bans. "What is with the casual clothes?" I teased.

He'd been on-site all night and morning and was ready to go get suited up. We would catch up at the press riser. "You are with the president today," he said. It was not a question.

I made my way over to the *Fox & Friends* crew. I was on with then-host Pete Hegseth; we did two segments and the rally-goers around him were exuberant. I interviewed several more people and then made my way toward the metal detectors.

Once officially inside, I sighed deeply. I was here. I made it on time and through the metal detectors; my anxiety was gone. I wasn't nervous about the pending interview, but oh, those logistics get me in the gut every time. Shannon was not with me this time;

Graeme Jennings, my colleague from the *Washington Examiner*, had driven up for the interview.

I saw Sean Parnell, a veteran Army Ranger and war hero who had spoken at the last Butler rally and was scheduled to speak today. A one-time candidate for Congress, he'd been only feet from Corey Comperatore when he was shot. We hugged.

"This place is unreal, right?" he asked, as we looked around us. "It feels like a revival."

He was not wrong.

I was one of the first reporters to arrive at the riser, and I was struck by what I saw in the stands: Comperatore's Buffalo Township firefighter's jacket and helmet were displayed in the top left corner of the stands, where Corey had been sitting when he was killed months earlier, surrounded by an arrangement of roses and gladioli.

The imagery was gut wrenching.

A few minutes later, a man walked onto the stage to practice for his appearance later that day—it was acclaimed tenor Christopher Macchio, who sang "Ave Maria" several times. I looked over at Corey's fire jacket and then at Macchio. I glanced around at all the people who had returned to Butler that day. Honestly, that takes guts. Tears welled up, but then I heard behind me the booming voice of Donald Gilliland, my former editor at the *Pittsburgh Tribune Review*, calling my name.

Now the politics editor at the *Pittsburgh Post-Gazette*, Gilliland and Sandra Tolliver, who was also my editor at the *Trib*, were my mentors. I could not tell you what Gilliland's political persuasion is, even though we've talked weekly for ten years. We have spoken a lot lately, trying to figure out this election cycle as we questioned the ineptitude of the Harris campaign. We were resigned to whatever she was doing as "the new normal" and not working.

The riser started to fill up with reporters. I saw *New York Times* reporter Maggie Haberman—we had both worked together at CNN, where she stayed on after I left. She looked around. It was her first time in Pennsylvania this cycle, and it was hard for her to deny that something big was happening here.

Slippery Rock mayor Jondavid Longo, Beaver County Republican Committee cochair Rico Elmore, and Scott Pressler, the tireless activist who singlehandedly registered thousands of Pennsylvania voters this cycle, all stopped by the riser to say hello.

Trump's plane flew over the Butler Farm Show Complex, and the crowd went wild. By now, there were well over sixty thousand people there, and it still would be over an hour before he arrived. He had to land at Pittsburgh International and ride in a motorcade to the rally.

The buzz at the Farm Show Complex rose to the next level.

Picard returned, wearing his suit. "You ready?"

We walked to the buffer with Jennings accompanying us. There, I saw photojournalists Evan Vucci, Doug Mills, and Anna Moneymaker. Mills and I hugged for a long time.

"You doing okay?" I asked him. He nodded. We were both quietly feeling the moment in our own ways, but I saw the emotion flicker in his eyes. I went over to Anna, and we embraced; the last time I saw her was when she was quietly crying behind the stage after the shooting.

Evan and I shook hands like we had just finished playing each other in a rugby match. That's Evan.

Picard brought me to the back of the stage where there were haystacks and several chicken coops. *Pretty funny background*, I thought. Steven Cheung, Trump's trusted aide, and Jason Miller, who has been with the president for an equally long time, were there for the handoff.

Cheung is traditionally all business and stoic. I got a smile and a hug. Miller gave me one as well. I turned to Cheung: "How is he about being here?"

"Good. He's good."

I saw Suzie Wiles, as always perfectly coifed, wearing a soft pink suit jacket over a fuchsia blouse. LaCivita was also on point, and he gave me a bear hug. Trump was in the curtained-off click room. I saw his son Eric (with his wife Lara), who has been his second at the Republican National Committee for this cycle. Like his father, Eric was wearing a suit and Lara was dressed in an emerald-green knit suit; she looked even more stunning in person.

J. D. Vance was standing outside the click room, where the ground had gone from being covered with a mesh tarp to dirt and grass—mostly dirt. We hugged as well. I realized then that I hug *a lot*. I blame that on my Italian-ness.

"How do you feel being here?" I asked him.

"It is obviously a little bittersweet," Vance said. "Bitter because Corey Comperatore is not with us, but sweet because there's so much energy and people are so excited. Obviously, you're kind of celebrating the fact the president is still here with us. I just spoke in a lot of rallies—none of them has been quite this emotional, none where I've seen the crowd this fired up."

I asked how he felt after his recent debate with Walz.

"Well, you never know, right? Your adrenaline's going, you're nervous, you're trying to just not sound like an idiot on national television, but the minute when I realized it had gone really well is my wife," he said. "One of her great character traits, but also something maybe I wish I could change, is that she cannot lie to me. And when I saw her face, I knew that I had done well, because she was so excited."

Next, I saw Helen Comperatore, Corey's wife, quietly moving out from the backstage area and making her way toward an
entrance into the stands. Cheung and Miller led me into the
curtained-off room where Trump was. He had just walked into
the room himself, after being with Helen, and he was wiping off
a smudge of dirt on his trousers that must have come from the
muddy ground outside the click room.

There were royal-blue curtains all around us, several American
flags, a red carpet where people had been standing with Trump for
photos, and something I don't usually see in these private areas:
mesh flooring covering the entire area.

"Salena, can you see that?" Trump asked about the dirt smudge.
I mean, I couldn't lie because, well, he's the former president of the
United States.

"Yes, but I don't think anyone else will. You will be behind the
podium," I assured him. I stared at the smudge, and now it was all
I could see. Surprisingly, he took my word for it and let it go.

I could tell by the sequence of the music playing that we didn't
have much time to chat.

Margo Martin, one of Trump's aides who has worked for him
for years, said, "Let's take a photo."

I stood beside him. He looked at me, put his thumb up, and we
laughed.

"How are you, Salena? My beautiful Salena," he asked. I laughed
again. Only my parents call me beautiful, but I'll take it.

"How are we doing here? I did good, yeah?" he asked about the
crowd.

"Really good."

Trump asked me if I had seen the polls that day, which showed
his popularity with Hispanic voters. He had taken the lead and
was pleased. It was getting close to "go time."

"Come on, let's ask me some questions. Let's walk toward the stage."

So, I asked, "How did you feel about this event when you flew over? What'd you think?"

"First of all, the crowd is massive. They said it was over one hundred thousand. Can you believe it? And we're in the middle of not a highly populated area," Trump said.

"It's those forty-two miles between here and East Palestine, Ohio, where I said everything changed for you when you showed up there," I told him.

Trump stopped walking and appeared to consider that. "Yeah."

"Everything changed," I continued. "You walked around in those galoshes, in the rain." We started walking again, and Wiles, Miller, and Eric and Lara Trump joined us.

"The other ones never showed up," he said.

I pointed out that *he* showed up for the people there.

"And I showed up to North Carolina and Georgia," he said of the flood-ravaged Appalachian region that was devastated by Hurricane Helene in September 2024, which destroyed entire towns. Biden and Harris were slow to respond to the storm damage, both rhetorically and with relief money from the Federal Emergency Management Agency—a misstep that would continue for months afterward and become as symbolic of government indifference in Appalachia as the response to the East Palestine rail disaster.

"I was in North Carolina—what a sight," Trump said. "I told reporters when they asked about winning North Carolina that I was there not to talk about votes; I was there to talk about my people. And I meant it. *I meant it.*"

He added, "North Carolina's been hit so hard and they tell me, the people will tell me, they don't see anybody even from the federal government."

We talked about Appalachia, and it made him think about J. D.

"I hear J. D. Vance made a good speech," he said of Vance's address to the Butler crowd moments before.

"I heard it was great, and Elon is speaking tonight with me," Trump said of billionaire businessman Elon Musk, who had become his staunch supporter.

We were walking again and had reached the stage entrance. I told Trump I'd like to meet Musk one day.

"Oh, you'll meet him," he said and turned to Miller. "Is Elon backstage or is he . . ."

Miller pointed to Musk, who was standing just ahead of us.

"Come on, come with me."

Trump stopped to glance at the monitor showing several different vantage points of the rally.

"So emotional today," he said, and I agreed. I saw the same look on his face that he had at the convention: grateful. Maybe a little out of sorts that he had survived this. He looked down at the smudge on his pants.

"Come on back with us, Salena. I think I'll stay off this stuff," he said of the mud.

"Well, that's why I wore my cowboy boots, sir," I joked. People often recognize me by my red, white, and blue cowboy boots.

"You're better off," he said with a laugh.

"Do you feel emotional today?" I asked.

Trump stopped walking. "I do," he admitted. "I don't want to think too much about it, because it's too tough. But I do."

"You know we're honoring Corey," he said then.

Trump looked back at the monitor. "Let me just see how we're doing here. Nobody's going to see that little spot on the pants, are they?"

"No," I told him again.

"How do we look, Salena?" he asked.

"You look fabulous. How do you feel?"

"I feel good."

"Do you know you're not the first president to ever be shot in Butler County?" I asked him.

"Who was?"

"George Washington."

"Oh, really? Well, that's a good one," he said.

"Right on the same side that you were."

"You've got to be kidding! Do you think that's maybe an omen?"

We had moved to his table with the hairspray. I knew what was coming.

"You want a little hair—"

I cut him off before he could finish the question. "No, I have too much hair."

We both cracked up. He looked down at the smudge of dirt again.

"Okay, that's okay. This is good. I'm ready. I think we're fine, right?"

Miller told him he looked good.

I joked that he looked beautiful.

"Best you can do. Best you can do. Come on. So, am I ready to go? Let's go," Trump said, then explained to me that he would be doing a ten-second moment of silence for Comperatore. "During that moment of silence, I have the best opera singer in the country. He's unbelievable. He's the best guy in the country. My brother's favorite, and he's going to sing 'Ave Maria' during the ten-second moment of silence. Do you like the idea?"

I am Catholic, so of course I love it. I told him, "That is powerful. I love it."

"Love it? And that's the right song, right?" Trump asked. He really wanted to honor Corey properly. It was clear his death has haunted him—that was a bullet meant for him, he had told me repeatedly the day after he was shot.

"At the end of the rally he will come back, and he'll do more songs. Wait 'til you hear this guy," he said. I asked if he wanted to make opera great again in this country. He smiled; I could tell he was thinking about that.

"I think you'll like this. Let me know afterwards. Call me tomorrow; let me know what you think," Trump said.

Elon Musk was beside the stage entrance. He walked over to Trump with a broad smile, clearly very excited to be part of the event.

"They said you wanted to talk to me," Musk said to Trump.

"Yes. This is a great friend of ours, Salena Zito," he said.

We shook hands. "Hi, how do you do?"

"Nice to meet you."

"She's the best writer on this part of the world, like the Rust Belt. The Pennsylvania Rust Belt," Trump said, adding, "She feels very good about our chances. I think I can say, right?"

"Yes," I told him.

"We're going to win North Carolina. We're going to win Pennsylvania," Musk said.

"She knows more about it than anybody. She's the best writer on what you call the Rust Belt, I think."

"We need a new name," Musk said. "Rust Belt's a terrible name."

I asked Musk if I could interview him, and he said sure. As we went back and forth for a story I would report the next day, Musk and Trump were also going back and forth, and it was evident that they had a bond.[1]

"He provided Starlink in North Carolina—they had no service," Trump interjected, apropos of nothing.

I asked Musk why he came to Butler today.

"The reason I'm here is because I think this is the most important election in our lifetime. I think President Trump represents the actual path to a democratic future, ironically, because they say he's a threat to democracy. But, in fact, the ones saying he's a threat to democracy are the ones who are a threat to democracy in reality," Musk said.

I asked him about the irony of that.

"Who are the ones that are trying to silence free speech? That's the Democrats," he said. "They're the ones trying to silence free speech. You know who the bad guys are—the ones who want to stop you from speaking. Those are the bad guys. It's a no-brainer."

He continued, "America is about freedom and opportunity. You have to have freedom to speak your mind. Why is the First Amendment, why does it exist? Because countries people came from, you'd get arrested or killed for speaking your mind. Why is the Second Amendment there? Because you weren't allowed to own firearms in other countries so they could oppress you. The thing protecting the First Amendment is the Second Amendment."

Trump had been studying the two of us and now interjected again.

"Salena, he's worth $300 billion. Salena, *$300 billion*. I worked my ass off and I'm like a fraction," Trump joked.

"If it wasn't for President Trump, this would be hopeless. Thank you," Musk said to him.

The interview with Musk occurred just out of happenstance or perhaps because Trump wanted me to interview him; a big part of me expects that is true. It is the only print interview Musk would do that cycle.

Country singer Lee Greenwood had walked onto the stage. Trump looked at me. "Thanks, Salena."

Less than a minute later, Picard ushered me into the buffer zone. I looked around. It was laid out differently from the last time I was here. There was a Plexiglas shield in front of Trump's podium.

Greenwood started his song, and Trump began to walk onto the stage. I looked over at Helen Comperatore in the front row; tears were staining her face. I looked at J. D. Vance, his wife Usha, Elon Musk, Eric and Lara Trump; they, too, were teary-eyed. The roar of the crowd seemed to go on forever, and many people were singing along with Lee Greenwood: "I'm proud to be an American, where at least I know I'm free . . ." Now Trump was standing right in front of me as I crouched down in the buffer area. His eyes were wet as well.

He stepped to the microphone and began, "As I was saying," a reference to that fateful day in July when a would-be assassin had interrupted his speech.

Those four words told everyone—perhaps even more so than when he raised his fist toward the crowd shouting, "Fight, fight, fight!" a moment after he was shot—that he is a man who will not be knocked down and is willing to leave everything on the field to take care of unfinished business in the White House. I remember reporting this at the time.

Then he turned to the man he did not want anyone to forget: "There's a hero who could not make it back here tonight, because he is no longer with us. Our beautiful Corey is not with us tonight, and he should be. We all miss him. He's become somewhat of a folk hero. Comperatore was an incredible husband and father, a devout Christian, a veteran, and a proud former fire chief—very respected within the town. Few men volunteer to run into fires, but Corey was one of those who did."

He described the last moments of Comperatore's life as leaping "into the fire one more time," by using his body to shield his family.

Trump asked everyone to join him in a moment of silence, and the melancholy strains of "Ave Maria" filled the air. When the singer had finished, Trump said, "God bless you, Corey. God bless you," adding that Comperatore was indeed on the stage in a "truly immortal position."

He spoke for two hours, a speech filled with emotion and grace, and at the end, Musk's remarks left the crowd feeling buoyed.

The next day, the media put forth several think pieces about the absurdity of working-class voters of any race or age being buoyed by Elon Musk. They just didn't get it, in the same way they didn't understand what was portended when Trump rode down the Trump Tower escalator in 2015. They did not grasp the connection that two billionaires could have with the country's working and middle class.

Musk, like Trump, is a risk-taker and builder, I explained in a story the next day, and that is something that appeals to the American psyche. People forget, but one of the things that helped Trump when he first ran for president was his ability to get things done.

Musk is the classic self-made billionaire. Paul Sracic, political science professor at Youngstown State University, explained to me: "He made his initial fortune by helping to design PayPal, an innovative online payment system that was later purchased by eBay. Rather than sit on his wealth, or just try to grow it by investing in the stock market, Musk used it to build other things. In almost every case, Musk's innovations paralleled things the government was trying to do, but he did it better."[2]

Think of it this way: the Inflation Reduction Act tries to use government subsidies to encourage companies to build, and consumers to buy electric vehicles, while Musk makes the vehicles.

For the past sixty years, one of the symbols of American inge-
nuity and world dominance has been the space program run by
the National Aeronautics and Space Administration (NASA), a
government agency. Sracic said, "Over the years, NASA has begun
contracting out its rocket program to private companies. One of
those companies, Boeing, was supposed to transport our astronauts back and forth to the International Space Station on their
Starliner capsule. When that capsule was found to have potential
safety issues, trapping two US astronauts on the Space Station for
months, it was Musk's SpaceX that rescued them."

The "revival" in western Pennsylvania never waned. Within two
weeks of the second rally in Butler, Trump was greeted with bois-
terous support when he attended a Pittsburgh Steelers game.

Then, spurred by an October 22 *Atlantic* story written by Jeffrey
Goldberg, former Trump chief of staff John Kelly said a day later
that Trump fits the definition of fascist.[3]

It would become the closing argument against Trump used by
Harris, the Democrats, and many in the mainstream media.

Chapter 11

"There Will Never Be Another One Like Him . . ."

FEASTERVILLE, *Pennsylvania*

It was like straddling two worlds.

One day after *Atlantic* magazine editor-in-chief Jeffrey Goldberg penned a story under the headline "Trump: 'I Need the Kind of Generals That Hitler Had': The Republican Nominee's Preoccupation with Dictators, and His Disdain for the American Military, Is Deepening," Trump was in Bucks County putting on an apron for a day's work at a local McDonald's franchise.[1]

The streets leading to the fast-food restaurant were lined with thousands of supporters. This was in a county that had gone for Hillary Clinton in 2016 and Joe Biden in 2020 and, in between, had also supported Democratic senator John Fetterman and Governor Josh Shapiro.

Goldberg, with whom I had appeared on several panels of CBS News' *Face the Nation*, dedicated five thousand words—as did the

New York Times—on John Kelly, Trump's former chief of staff who, as the *Times* paraphrased, said: "Trump met the definition of a fascist, would govern like a dictator if allowed, and had no understanding of the Constitution or the concept of rule of law."[2]

The mood outside the McDonald's was festive. Some protesters had shown up to taunt the Trump supporters, but the jawing back and forth was minimal as Trump worked the deep fryer at his favorite fast-food chain.

It was the ultimate troll, first because he loves McDonald's and he knows most Americans also do, but second, because he was also trolling Vice President Kamala Harris, who said she had worked at a McDonald's in California after her freshman year of college but never provided evidence of that employment.

The press and Democrats groaned, but if you were there, it was quite the move—Paul Sracic, the political scientist from Youngstown State, said in a story reported that day that if you followed the event on social media with clear eyes, you could see Trump was having fun—and so was everyone watching it. "A lot of the coverage out of the gate after the convention about Harris was this forced message about joy," Sracic said. "You cannot watch this guy, the former president of the United States, waiting on people at the drive-thru window and not kind of smile at it."[3]

In that moment, Trump wasn't just relatable; "he was able to poke fun at himself," Sracic said.

For the next ten days, mainstream news outlets such as the *New York Times*,[4] the *Atlantic*, the *Washington Post*,[5] *Politico*,[6] and *Axios*[7] published articles repeating the charge that Trump was a fascist.

It filled social media platforms. Cable news grabbed it: Kamala Harris called Trump a fascist on CNN.[8] On MSNBC's *Morning Joe*, hosts Joe Scarborough and his wife Mika Brzezinski said he had fascist rhetoric.[9] Billionaire entrepreneur and television personality Mark Cuban echoed that Trump "absolutely" has "fascist tendencies."[10]

When Trump announced that he would hold a campaign event at Madison Square Garden, he was compared to Hitler because, eighty years earlier, a pro-Nazi rally had been held there. Never mind that Franklin Delano Roosevelt had held a campaign rally there, as had Lyndon Baines Johnson in 1964 and Bill Clinton—all Democrats.

The *New York Times'* coverage of Trump's rally at Madison Square Garden called the event "a release of rage at a political and legal system that impeached, indicted and convicted him, a vivid and at times racist display of the dark energy animating the MAGA movement."[11]

There were nine days left before the election, and the view from the *Times* was that Trump was closing a toss-up race that he now could lose because of "a carnival of grievances, misogyny and racism."

The outrage was focused on an insult comic who had called Puerto Rico a "floating island of garbage." Kamala Harris immediately issued a statement saying that Trump "fans the fuel of hate and division" before she flew to Michigan for a campaign event. Joe Biden called the rally "simply embarrassing."[12]

It always amazes me how many think pieces can emerge within minutes of an event. Did these reporters go out and talk to voters? Seems unlikely. More likely, they picked up a phone and texted an activist to get the answer they wanted for the story—to support a premise they thought should be happening, not what was happening.

The outrage machine was churning out stories. According to the Associated Press, the *New York Times*, and the *Washington Post*, Trump stood to lose not only Puerto Rican voters but also his support among all Hispanic voters.

I was not convinced.

Holly Otterbein penned a piece in *Politico* with two other reporters, with the initial headline (later changed): "Donald Trump Has a Serious Puerto Rico Problem—in Pennsylvania!" They reported, "Many Puerto Rican voters in the state are furious about racist and demeaning comments delivered at a Trump rally." That dismay was giving Harris an opening to win over all of the state's Hispanic voters, especially the nearly half-million Pennsylvanians of Puerto Rican descent in Allentown—the city Trump was set to visit on Tuesday.[13]

Otterbein said her evidence of a backlash came from Puerto Rican voters who were lighting up WhatsApp chats and commenting in morning conversations at their bodegas. She added there were plans for a protest at Trump's rally in Allentown, which is home to one of the largest Puerto Rican populations in the state.

I was skeptical. I had talked to many Hispanic people in Berks County and the Lehigh Valley for decades about traditional values, faith, and family. Hispanic voters in Pennsylvania had been moving to the right for a long time, and Trump was accelerating that shift.

The arena where Trump was speaking was in the middle of the city's Puerto Rican neighborhood, so I got there early and camped out to talk to voters.

There was a massive crowd, many of Puerto Rican descent, but they weren't there to protest; they were in line to see Trump. As for the "big protest" against Trump, there was technically one about a block away from the event, with a few dozen people organized by Make the Road Action, which describes itself as the "largest Latinx organization in the state."

I found no Hispanic Allentown resident who ever referred to themselves as Latinx. Instead, what I found outside PPL Center were Trump supporters of all races happily waiting in line to get in.

Nothing had changed.

At the same time this event was going on, two hundred miles straight down Interstate 95, people were waiting for Kamala Harris to speak at the Ellipse, a park in the nation's capital. Unbeknownst to Harris, who was inside the White House, President Joe Biden was calling Trump supporters "garbage" on a Zoom call.[14]

In that moment, three things that were supposed to go one way went in an entirely different direction, nearly all at the same time. Harris expected to have reporters give her glowing reviews for her dark speech attacking Donald Trump from the same place where he gave his controversial "challenge the election" speech on January 6, 2021. Trump expected to have to navigate the fallout from a cheeky joke by an insult comic. And Biden expected to continue to attack Trump on that issue on a Zoom call.

Nothing went as planned.

Instead of invoking a contrast to Trump and giving people a compelling reason to vote for her, Harris reminded voters that she works in the White House, a place most voters agreed had led the country down the wrong track for the past four years.

Brad Todd, a CNN contributor and Republican media strategist, told me that the choice of Harris standing with the White House illuminated behind her was political malpractice.[15]

Said Todd, "Sixty-eight percent of Americans think that the country is on the wrong track, and they blame Joe Biden, and increasingly, they are blaming Kamala Harris. By standing in front of the White House, she is going to own all 68 percent of that disapproval."

Harris also suffered from Biden's sucking all the air out of the room as reporters scrambled to cover his remark that half the people in the country were "garbage."

As if on cue, national political reporters shamelessly and without conscience told the nation that Biden hadn't really called Trump supporters garbage.

Jonathan Lemire at *Politico* said the Biden quote was taken out of context.[16] The *New York Times* said it "appeared" Biden said it, and plenty of people on X claimed that Biden didn't say what Biden did say.[17]

Trump supporters with whom I talked were still in "revival mode." They joked in our interviews that they weren't sure if they were supposed to be fascists, Hitler supporters, or just plain garbage.[18]

After years of being referred to as bitter, clinging to their guns and Bibles, irredeemable deplorables, racists, and extremists, everybody with whom I spoke believed that Biden meant it the way it sounded—and nobody was surprised by it.

What I had expected to write about that day was what happened in Allentown: Did Trump invoke the wrath of the local Puerto Rican community over a joke from an insult comedian? Was there a visible sign of anger from the community? Were people switching their votes? Did they protest? Was Trump contrite?

What happened instead was that Biden stole the limelight, and, no matter how hard the national press tried to cover for him, his use of "garbage" had a negative resonance.

On the drive home, I was struck by how quickly the garbage quip stuck. People had placed Trump signs on their garbage cans outside. Everywhere I stopped, people were talking about Biden's remark. That night was Halloween, and I could count on two hands the number of people I saw wearing either garbage bags, orange safety vests, or McDonald's uniforms as costumes.

For added measure, Trump jumped in a garbage truck in Michigan and drove it around. My goodness, he makes it look so easy to play them.

It was over in Pennsylvania. By my calculations, likely by about two percentage points, or around 175,000 people. I wrote the story the next day, saying, "Whoever wins here will also win Michigan,

Wisconsin, North Carolina, Arizona, Georgia, and Nevada because Pennsylvania is a bit more Democrat than those states."[19]

My boss bet me a shot of whiskey that I was wrong. I told him I prefer tequila.

I was not wrong. I went on CNN, Fox News, and several podcasts stating my opinion, despite the last-minute Ann Selzer poll out of Iowa saying that Harris was within striking distance of Trump.

Selzer is an icon in the polling world. She has done the *Des Moines Register* poll since 1997, and her predictions rarely miss. It was the Saturday before the election and, for whatever reason, she found Harris and Trump neck and neck—a shocking result in Iowa, a state not considered to be competitive.

No way, I told my boss. I never had a sliver of a doubt.

I called Wes Anderson, the pollster at OnMessage Public Strategies. We often rely on each other, though we come from very different worlds—he is all data and spreadsheets, and I am all people and place. We agreed this was a, well, garbage poll.

"Trump wins by two percent, you think?" I asked him.

"Yup, two percent," he said.

On Monday, Trump headed to Pittsburgh. The Biden garbage remark had taken on a life of its own. Shannon and I went to PPG Paints Arena for the event. We would not be interviewing Trump this time, so we didn't need to get there too early. We parked in a back parking lot by Duquesne University to avoid the potential crowd. We had no idea what kind of crowd Trump would draw in Pittsburgh, a city that has traditionally been Democratic territory.

We cut across several parking lots in the Hill District and then turned on Forbes Avenue, where we were astonished by what we saw. A line of rally-goers wound all the way up to the Oakland neighborhood, well over a mile, packed with people of all ages.

We saw a healthy mix of young people, including not just white individuals but also Asian, Hispanic, and Black.

We walked the five blocks to the entrance, listening to music filling the streets: "God Bless America" and "YMCA." We ran into photojournalist Justin Merriman, who said we'd have to go three blocks up Center Avenue to get into the press entrance.

When we turned the corner to walk up that street, it was packed for another mile.

"Are you sure we are going to the right place?" Shannon joked. When we entered the arena, a paramedic pulled me aside and said, "Hey, aren't you Ron Zito's daughter?"

Yes, I told him.

"Hey, tell him I said hi. I was the paramedic who took him to the hospital when he broke his back trying to put up his flagpole for his American flag."

We took a photo together, and I texted it to my dad. That is Pittsburgh for you. I am convinced there is zero degree of separation between all of us. To add to the sense of connection, the Hill District is the neighborhood my immigrant Italian family first settled in when they arrived in this country separately as children. The neighborhood was poor, Black, Italian, Jewish, and very close-knit; my grandparents met on the very spot where PPG Paints Arena was built. They married one block north and owned their first home here as well.

Inside, the place filled up quickly. We were standing in the press riser when Tim Murtaugh, the spitting-image grandson of the great Pittsburgh Pirates player-turned-World Series manager Danny Murtaugh, came up to me.

Tim had been LaCivita's protégé for twenty years and a trusted member of Trump's communication team. "Salena, I want to show you someone," he said and led me by the hand to the seats closest to the stage. There in the front row was Roberto Clemente Jr. *My God, he looks like his dad*, I thought.

I looked over at Murtaugh, who shared a striking resemblance to the man who had coached Clemente's father. He had tears in his eyes.

Pirates right-fielder Roberto Clemente is Pittsburgh royalty. He embodied all that was good in us and more, and his legendary work ethic, talent, and generosity of spirit have been revered here since he tragically died in a plane crash on December 31, 1972, while on a humanitarian mission.

He was the son of Puerto Rico. His son, Roberto Jr., was as well, and he is well-respected in Pittsburgh. His endorsement of Trump was a big deal. Shannon took his photo, and I tweeted out the story.[20]

The narrative that Puerto Rican voters won't support Trump died in that moment.

———

When Election Day dawned the next morning, I was booked to do several hits on Fox News. Each time, I remained firm in my contention that Trump would win Pennsylvania by two percentage points.

As a result, my phone was blowing up all day with the same four words in each text: "What are you hearing?"

I had been invited to Florida to cover Trump's election night event, but that didn't seem right—I needed to be in Pennsylvania where it mattered.

Shannon, Michael, and I headed downtown to the Fairmont Hotel, where Republican Senate candidate David McCormick would hold a victory party for his Senate race as well as the Trump victory party for Allegheny County.

The place was packed when we arrived. I ran into the local public news reporter whose name I can never remember. He came up to me and said, "I got a bone to pick with you about your Trump story last night. In Pittsburgh there wasn't that many young people."

Our quick conversation—mostly his rant about why I was wrong—was luckily interrupted by Brad Todd, who had just arrived from Alexandria, Virginia. He came to Pittsburgh because he was running McCormick's race. Although we wrote a book together, talk frequently, and are very close, I had not seen him in person since 2020. Bear hugs! He allowed me to come to the McCormick war room if I would be a fly on the wall and stay out of everyone's way.

Shannon and Mike left; they had four kids at home.

I found myself a spot on the floor in the war room. McCormick was there with his wife Dina Powell, his communications person, Elizabeth Gregory, along with Brad and Mark Harris, McCormick's other top strategist.

No one thought McCormick would beat Senator Bob Casey Jr. The Scranton Democrat with a legacy name (his father was Pennsylvania's forty-second governor) has been in office for forty years and had a ton of campaign money. But I knew differently—I thought McCormick would win, though not by as big a margin as Trump.

I was watching the results from Erie, Luzerne, Northampton, and Bucks Counties—the ones I knew would matter most. One by one, Trump was winning them; it was not even close. He was winning them far beyond 2016 numbers. By 10:00 p.m., I knew he'd won Pennsylvania. The Associated Press did not call the race here until 2:24 a.m. EST. Soon after, it called Wisconsin, Michigan, North Carolina, Georgia, Nevada, and Arizona.

My boss owed me some tequila.

While I had reported out of all those states this year, it was Pennsylvania that told the story of all of them—and, more importantly, America's working class told the ultimate story.

At the end of the day, people like cosmetologist Autumn Colamarino from Apollo, waitress Angela Wade from Greensburg, and janitor Douglas Holman from Penn Hills, who aspired to be a sportswriter, were among those who decided this election, not the highly educated scolds but the people who make this country move and make our lives better.

I left the Fairmont Hotel at 4:00 a.m. I had watched Trump earlier in Florida, with his family, and as he took the stage, I saw that expression on his face again. It's fleeting, but it appears he still can't believe he's here. He has said that to me several times since July 13. He's grateful.

One thing I knew for certain: there will never be another one like him.

If you wanted to have a keen, dispassionate understanding of how much the Republican Party has changed over the past eight years, all you had to do was stand outside PPG Paints Arena in the city's Hill District neighborhood and see the line of people stretching ten blocks in either direction up Fifth Avenue. Or attend the rallies in Allentown, Philadelphia, or Butler.

Many of the attendees were young men and women, and there were Black, white, Hispanic, and Asian people all having a great time, getting to know each other, singing songs in line, swapping stories about where they were from, and almost always finding out they shared a mutual friend.

They were never what others in my profession wrote about them.

Inside each event venue, a keen observer could witness the emergence of a new coalition of Republican voters that I had been reporting about for the past few years: union workers, nurses, janitors, businessmen and women, doctors, lawyers, police officers, and college students of every race and generation.[21] They were there because of their support for Donald Trump. However, they were there more for their support for each other.

There will never be another candidate for president of the United States like Trump, I wrote, because it was what I heard from so many voters.[22]

For his detractors, that is a relief. However, they should understand that whether Trump wins or loses, these voters are here to stay. They have seen what the power of the cultural curators in our country—in academia, media, Hollywood, institutions, corporations, and bureaucracies—has done to their lives, and they have rejected it.

It took someone as brash, unconventional, strong, and cheeky as Trump to be the bull in the china shop, and his supporters wanted to see things upended. They wanted someone who, when shot, would stand up and say, "Fight, fight, fight!"

The elites had mocked them for too long. The elites tried to change their values and their children's values. The elite movies insulted them. The elite reporting was biased against them. The universities had lost credibility, and the corporations had decided to dump decades of loyalty to them to satisfy a narrow consumer base I reported on the final day.[23]

This will come as a surprise to some, but Trump did not create this coalition. He is the result of it. That is what the people who want the Republican Party to be the party of Dick Cheney again do not understand. Both parties have changed. Republicans are now the party of working-class Americans, and Democrats are the party of the elites.

When Trump came down that escalator nine years ago, my profession focused on something he said about Mexican people. I have written endlessly for the past nine years that what journalists missed and every working-class person heard was a speech he gave on the dignity of work—a speech that was not much different from the one Bill Clinton delivered in 1992 when he announced he was running for president.[24] But Trump's speech was delivered in an unconventional way that people would see for the next eight years.

Why did so many voters like it? Because Democrats and Republicans have been delivering beautiful oratory for decades, and none of those slurpy words made anyone's lives better. None of their words helped their communities or their schools, or provided them opportunities—that is, unless you had wealth and power.[25]

The emotion was palpable in Pittsburgh's arena on the Monday night before Election Day. It was a continuum of the ardor in Butler. Of everything that happened in Butler—the taking of the life of an everyman, the failure of the Secret Service to protect a former president—symbolic of the failure of all our institutions. People knew when they left Butler the first time that they had been part of something they might never see again.

Political affiliations often defy logic. Since the 1930s, the Democrats have acted like they owned the working-class voter with good reason: they did. Trump's style upended that. Sometimes to Trump's detriment, sometimes to his advantage, this coalition that Brad Todd and I detailed in our book *The Great Revolt: Inside the Populist Coalition Reshaping American Politics* has only expanded.

And this coalition will go on. The old Republican Party is not getting back together for the foreseeable future. Neither is the Democratic Party. Coalitions move like tectonic plates—they change ever so slightly. Trump was the one who saw what was right in front of us and seized it. Because of his intuition, the Republican coalition coalesced, while the Democrats collapsed.

And with them, they took their cohorts in the American press.

Chapter 12

The Reckoning

BETHEL PARK, *Pennsylvania*

On July 13, 2024, a frantic Matthew Crooks picked up the phone in his suburban Pittsburgh home at 10:56 p.m. and called 911. The father of two said he was worried because his son, Thomas Matthew Crooks, had gone radio silent since midafternoon.

"Hi, yes. Uh, my name is Matthew Crooks. I was calling in regards to my son, Thomas. Uh, he belongs to the Clairton Sportsman Club." (This is the transcription from the 911 dispatch; it is the quirky way western Pennsylvania folks talk.)

Matthew Crooks also mentioned his son was twenty years old.

"The reason I'm calling is, he left the house here at about a quarter to two this afternoon, and we've gotten no contact from him, no text messages, nothing's been returned, and he's not home yet. That's totally not like him. So, we're kind of worried, not really sure what we should do."

Matthew Crooks placed the call nearly five hours after Donald Trump had been shot at a campaign rally in Butler, Pennsylvania.

ABC News reported that in the 911 recording, Crooks's voice was steady but sounded slightly tense.[1] The news report came out on December 5, 2024, marking the first time in months that anything had been reported about the Crooks family.

It took *ABC*'s national news desks five months to obtain the audio details from that call.

The news agency got the recording from an open records request to Allegheny County, where the Crooks family's Bethel Park home is located.

On that same day, the bipartisan US House of Representatives' Task Force on the Attempted Assassination of Donald J. Trump issued its report.[2]

Chaired by Butler County congressman Mike Kelly, a Republican, and Representative Jason Crow, a Colorado Democrat, the report found the Secret Service had failed Trump at the rally by enabling the chilling ease of access that Thomas Matthew Crooks had that day:

> The Task Force identified several decision points that, if handled differently, could have prevented Crooks from firing eight shots at the Butler rally stage.
>
> Foremost, the failure to secure a recognized high-risk area immediately adjacent to the venue—specifically the American Glass Research (AGR) grounds and building complex—gave rise to several vulnerabilities that eventually allowed Crooks to evade law enforcement, climb on and traverse the roof of the AGR complex, and open fire.
>
> Despite its proximity to a main road, clear sight lines to the stage, and elevated position, the Secret Service allowed a crowd that was not screened by USSS or other law enforcement to gather at the fence line separating the secured area and the AGR complex.

The presence of the crowd outside the secured area made Crooks more difficult to interdict as his behavior became increasingly suspicious.

The consequences of failing to secure the AGR property in the first place were compounded by the fact that the area was not sufficiently monitored or patrolled to deter threats.

The Secret Service did not provide clear guidance to its state and local partners about which entity was responsible for the area. An expressed lack of manpower and assets was not sufficiently addressed, resulting in coverage gaps on the ground. Further, local snipers on the property understood their responsibility to be over watch of the crowd and venue, not the area outside the secure perimeter where Crooks loitered and prepared, believing that area to have been secured by Secret Service counter-snipers and patrol units.

The result of that misunderstanding was that the local sniper team posted in the windows of one of the AGR buildings was not positioned to monitor the area directly underneath the windows or the roofs.

While another local sniper team stationed on the opposite side of the venue did have line of sight to the AGR property, they similarly did not believe they were responsible for monitoring the area and did not do so.

These issues were compounded by failures that arose on the day of the event.

Technology meant to supplement venue security was out of commission for hours. A fragmented communication structure and poor decision-making prevented vital information from reaching pertinent law enforcement personnel.

These technology and communication breakdowns hindered law enforcement's pursuit of Crooks and caused missed opportunities to intervene. The breakdowns also interrupted the flow of information that should have been passed to Secret Service personnel with the ability to remove the former President from the stage.

Moreover, relevant threat information known by members of the intelligence community was not escalated to key personnel working the rally.

The failures that led to the tragic events of July 13 were not entirely isolated to the campaign event itself, or the days preceding it.

Preexisting issues in leadership and training created an environment in which the specific failures identified above could occur.

Secret Service personnel with little to no experience in advance planning roles were given significant responsibility, despite the July 13 event being held at a higher-risk outdoor venue with many line-of-sight issues, in addition to specific intelligence about a long-range threat.

Further, some of the Secret Service agents in significant advance planning roles did not clearly understand the delineation of their responsibilities.

In total, the 180-page, 35,000-word report named Crooks only ten times.

For Representative Mike Kelly, this wasn't just his job as a member of Congress; this was personal.

Kelly had been at the rally that day. And Butler, well, Butler is special to him: It's his hometown. His family business, which his father founded, is located there.

He had been sitting in the front row, and Corey Comperatore, the firefighter who was fatally shot, was seated behind him. Corey was one of Kelly's constituents.

Just days after the report came out, Kelly returned home to Butler. We talked about the report's findings and the election. Kelly, who attended Notre Dame on a football and athletic scholarship, is still an imposing man with a shock of white hair and a booming voice that has been part of his appeal to voters in this one-time Democratic-leaning congressional seat.

Kelly said if there was one way to sum up the shooting of a president, how the Secret Service's incompetence contributed, and the baffling lack of knowledge about Thomas Crooks, it is that the American people responded to what happened with their votes. "There will be a reckoning for our institutions and that includes our press. Sorry, Salena," he said. I'm good with that; I get it. "There has to be," he continued. "They have all failed us. And in many ways, that is what voters were telling us all along. The press saw it as resentment and grievances towards our institutions and the press. I disagree. It isn't resentment and it is not anger; it really isn't. It is a message of, we have lost confidence in you, and you need to live up to your missions. You cannot put the genie back in the bottle. Nothing is going back to the way it was, in terms of confidence in what they do."

Kelly's task force has put the Secret Service on notice. But what about the press? Where were the deep dives into what happened? Where were the investigative reporters who would dig and dig until they got answers?

They aren't here anymore. Local newspapers have been hollowed out steadily for decades, or they've closed shop entirely. New, younger reporters are rewarded by their managers for producing short, aggregated news stories with provocative headlines that drive online clicks, rather than by a team of managing editors, city desk editors, and copy desk editors charged with making sure they got it right.

A couple of days before Trump won the 2024 presidential election, the online clubby news organization *Axios* declared: "The big media era is over." It noted that the "mainstream media's dominance in narrative- and reality-shaping in presidential elections shattered in 2024."[3]

It wasn't wrong.

The funny thing is, *Axios* is very much in the center of that "narrative- and reality-shaping" business. What has happened to my industry, and, more importantly, where will it go from here?

Not long ago, nearly every city, town, and rural area had its own news organization. These were usually owned by well-heeled benefactors in the community who ran a benevolent organization that provided a service to the community at large.

Newsrooms across the country were filled with local residents, some of whom did not have journalism degrees or had not even attended college, but they were go-getters, and they could write good copy. They had a knack for developing sources. They were culturally connected to the people in the community; in other words, they were one of them, coaching kids' ball teams, serving as ushers at church, or belonging to the local Elks Club.

If you were a local reporter and you got a story wrong, there were consequences. These reporters weren't perfect, but they were held accountable.

The biggest decline in local news organizations began in earnest in 2005—since then, more than 3,200 newspapers in America have folded, according to the Local News Initiative at Northwestern University's Medill School of Journalism.[4]

There are several hundred counties across this country, most of them rural, with no local news organizations, meaning they get their news from journalists who have no connection with their lives. If they cover something like religion or gun ownership, their news stories are often presented from an Ivy Leaguer's perspective of people of faith or people who own guns.

In 2020, *News-Gazette* publisher Matt Paxton told me in a story I did from Lexington, Virginia, that the reason people trust their small newspaper in Rockbridge County more than the national news is accountability regarding their stories.[5]

"We all have the experience of writing a story and then walking down the street and running into the person that we just wrote about," Paxton told me. "And when you write a story, you keep that in the back of your mind. You want to be scrupulously fair and not just throwing arrows."

Once the president of the National Newspaper Association, Paxton is bullish on the future of community newspapers despite all the bad news nationally. "No doubt, they are always needed and critical," he said. "They are the heart of where the trust in news lives."

The *News-Gazette* wasn't the only paper in this town. There was also the *Rockbridge Advocate*, with its quirky slogan: "Independent as a Hog on Ice."

Few journalists are more respected in the news business, old media and new, than Carl Cannon, the Washington bureau chief for *RealClearPolitics* and dean of American journalism. Much of that respect has to do with Cannon's evenhandedness throughout his long career and his adaptation to new media.

Cannon began his journalism career at age fourteen as a paperboy for the *San Francisco Chronicle*, delivering ninety newspapers over a five-mile radius on a bicycle stripped down for speed and lightness.

He recalled to me a story he wrote years ago about how he fell in love with the power of the delivery of news in 1968, a year when there was a *lot* of big news.[6] Minnesota senator Eugene McCarthy had given President Lyndon B. Johnson enough of a scare in the March 12 New Hampshire primary that Johnson announced he would not seek reelection.

Senator Robert F. Kennedy soon entered the race, and a month later, civil rights leader Martin Luther King Jr. was murdered. On the night of the California primary, Cannon went to bed early; he had to get up and deliver the paper at 5:45 a.m.

His mother awakened him at 4:30 the next morning. Bobby Kennedy had been shot in Los Angeles. Cannon's father, a newspaperman, had been at work all night but had called to ask that his son deliver the latest bulletin to customers.

Cannon told his mother no one would be awake, but his mother persisted. She told him that when they did wake up, they'd want to know what happened.

Cannon's mother was right. Almost every house he delivered to had its kitchen lights on. People saw him and opened their doors as he came to deliver the news. He recited the news his mother had written down on an index card for him to take with him.

A paper route that usually took one hour took three hours as he was greeted with hugs by grieving neighbors. The day left him with a searing appreciation for the power of news.

Cannon would go on to attend journalism school in Boulder, Colorado. His first job was at a weekly newspaper in nearby Longmont covering city council and school board meetings. As Cannon told me, "The guy who owned the paper, who was also the editor, would literally pay me five dollars in cash for each article. He'd open a drawer and hand me, like, ten bucks."

He loved reporting. He loved digging in. He loved seeing his byline in print. He wanted to do more, so every Saturday, he put on radio announcer Milton Cross with the New York Metropolitan City Opera, and for as long as it lasted, he wrote letters to newspaper editors and publishers across the country, hoping one of them would interview him for a job.

It took a while. His parents had moved to northern Virginia, so he relocated there and found work on a weekly newspaper, the *Reston Times*. For a few years, he bounced around among several newspapers, covering the cops beat, the courts, school boards— tough beats that taught him so much about the importance of good journalism.

He eventually ended up in Washington, DC, covering the 1984 presidential election, and then the White House from Ronald Reagan through Bill Clinton. Later he landed at *RealClearPolitics*, where he has been since 2011.

What Cannon learned from covering the cops beat is still instructive to him today. These lessons were no more apparent than when he covered the September 2024 *ABC News* debate between Donald Trump and Kamala Harris, and Trump cited the rise of violent crime as a criticism of the Biden-Harris administration's record.

"Crime here is up, and through the roof, despite their fraudulent statements that they made," Trump said during the debate. "Crime in this country is through the roof."

ABC debate moderator David Muir immediately issued Trump a fact-check, admonishing, "President Trump, *as you know*, the FBI says overall violent crime is actually coming down in this country."

Trump was having none of it. "Excuse me, they were defrauding statements. They didn't include the worst cities. They didn't include the cities with the worst crime. It was a fraud. Just like their number of 818,000 jobs that they said they created turned out to be a fraud."

Cannon knew Trump was right because he knew that cities like Chicago and my hometown of Pittsburgh and numerous other big cities weren't reporting their violent crimes to the FBI. Within days, the FBI updated its data to reflect the rise in crime.

As for *ABC News*? They never issued an apology or an update.

Cannon points to one of a thousand different cuts to credibility that his profession has self-inflicted. He knew about the FBI's *Uniform Crime Reports* and how inaccurate it is because of his time covering courts, matters that remain relevant but on which reporters rarely cut their teeth today.

Bias in journalism hasn't been directed just at Republicans—*RealClearPolitics* has been a target as well, and Cannon had a slow burn on a story done in 2020 that he let linger for four years. He'd hoped his beloved profession, one he shared with his father, as I shared with my grandfather, would self-correct. When Cannon saw the destructive direction the national press was crashing head-first into in 2024, he decided to write about it.[7]

His broadside to the national press as an institution revealed just how biased the national news had become.

Ten days after the 2020 election, Tom Bevan, co-founder and president of RealClearPolitics, received an email from a *New York Times* reporter who covers the media. The reporter, Jeremy W. Peters, advised Bevan that his newspaper was working on a story about RCP and asked for responses to various questions and accusations. Four days later, Peters' critique was published under the headline "A Popular Political Site Made a Sharp Right Turn. What Steered It."

The sleight-of-hand was right there in the headline. The *New York Times* simply declared that RCP "made a sharp right turn," and suggested it will document how this happened.

The Times' story asserted that during the period of counting absentee and late-arriving mail-in ballots, RCP took three days longer than other news organizations to call Pennsylvania for Joe Biden. It noted disapprovingly that we aggregated stories from other news outlets quoting Trump supporters who questioned the election results. It suggested that the RCP Poll Averages were manipulated to be favorable to Donald Trump. Peters focused on RCP staff layoffs in September 2017, and claimed we'd hired partisan Republicans to replace them. He reported that the Real-Clear Foundation, a nonprofit that supports our journalism, receives contributions from conservative donors. He also called into question a RealClear Investigations exposé naming the whistleblower whose complaints led to Trump's first impeachment.

Jeremy Peters declined to be interviewed for this rebuttal, though he was courteous about it. Nor did he reach out to me in 2020, beyond contacting Tom Bevan. It didn't hurt my pride, but I'm the most experienced newsman at RCP; I oversee our original content, I direct our reporters, and I have written more words for RealClear than anyone else.

Nor was there any bad blood between me and the "paper of record." In the 1980s, the Times credited my ground-breaking coverage of the Catholic Church sex abuse scandal.[8] In the 1990s, Howell Raines tried to hire me. Three books[9] I've co-authored have been positively reviewed by the Times.[10] When I covered the White House for National Journal, the Times' book editor asked me to review a book about Dick Cheney.[11] I have had friends at that newspaper. Although I'm not famous, I'm not unknown in Washington journalism.

What I'm best known for is being relentlessly nonpartisan. If someone is writing about bias at my organization, calling me would have been the obvious place to start.

BUTLER, Pennsylvania—Vietnam War veteran and local farmer Harry Norman, who served three tours of duty and twenty years total in the military, was attending his first political rally in his life. heading to sit by the stage. *(Photo by Shannon Venditti)*

BUTLER, Pennsylvania—A volunteer for the Donald Trump rally in Butler looks out on the bustling crowd as the first rallygoers file in to their seats and stands. *(Photo by Shannon Venditti)*

BUTLER, Pennsylvania—Rallygoers wait in the blistering heat on July 13 for then-candidate Donald Trump to take to the stage. *(Photo by Shannon Venditti)*

BUTLER, Pennsylvania—President Donald J. Trump approaches the stage in Butler to address the crowd. *(Photo by Shannon Venditti)*

BUTLER, Pennsylvania—Looking on to his loyal supporters, President Donald J. Trump makes his way to the podium in the summer heat. *(Photo by Shannon Venditti)*

BUTLER, Pennsylvania—The aftermath of the assassination attempt on the life of President Donald J. Trump left first responders on their toes. *(Photo by Shannon Venditti)*

BUTLER, Pennsylvania—The crowd was gone, the speakers were gone, but everything else—including wheelchairs, tables, food, cameras, hats—was left on the Butler County Fairgrounds' dirt in the wake of the assassination attempt on Donald J. Trump's life. *(Photo by Shannon Venditti)*

BUTLER, Pennsylvania—The media was kept in a safe spot during evacuation of the president and the crowds at the now-infamous Butler rally. Here, Salena Zito goes live on her first of many radio hits following the assassination attempt. *(Photo by Shannon Venditti)*

PITTSBURGH, Pennsylvania—J. D. Vance at the old
Pennsylvania Station in downtown Pittsburgh for a rally
two weeks before election day. Vance texts his mother, Bev
Aikens, before our interview to let her know Salena would be
interviewing her in Middletown in two days. *(Photo by Shannon
Venditti)*

KITTANNING, Pennsylvania—President Donald Trump speaks to both the media and Ryan Sprankle, the owner of Sprankles grocery store, as his campaign co-chair and future White House chief of staff Susie Wiles looks on. *(Photo by Shannon Venditti)*

BUTLER, Pennsylvania—On October 5, 2024, Donald Trump returns to the site of the assassination attempt for a rally that attendees said felt more like a revival. Corey Comperatore's Buffalo Township fireman's jacket and helmet were displayed in the top left corner of the stands, where Corey had been sitting when he was killed months earlier, surrounded by an arrangement of roses and gladioluses. The imagery was gut wrenching. *(Photo by Salena Zito)*

BUTLER, Pennsylvania—Salena Zito interviews Donald Trump during his return to Butler in October. After taking the stage, Trump stepped to the microphone and began, "As I was saying," a reference to that fateful day in July when a would-be assassin had interrupted his speech. *(Photo by Graeme Jennings)*

"The reason I'm here is because I think this is the most important election in our lifetime," billionaire Elon Musk tells Salena Zito at the October 5 return to Butler rally. It is the only print interview Musk will do that cycle. *(Photo by Graeme Jennings)*

HARRISBURG, Pennsylvania—The packed arena at Indiana University of Pennsylvania cheers on President Donald J. Trump. *(Photo by Shannon Venditti)*

HARRISBURG, Pennsylvania—Many Trump supporters waved their flags, wore their red MAGA caps, and even donned capes or themed costumes in support of the then-candidate Donald J. Trump. *(Photo by Shannon Venditti)*

I shouldn't have waited three years to respond to the Times but will do so now.[12]

Cannon went on to note that the thrust of the November 17, 2020, *New York Times* article was that *RealClearPolitics* had "taken a rightward, aggressively pro-Trump turn over the last four years," with Peters accusing *RCP* of giving "top billing" to stories reinforcing the "false narrative" that Trump could eke out a win.[13]

Cannon made a thorough audit of *RCP*'s archives of that cycle to see if Peters had an argument—as a good reporter, that's certainly what Peters should have done before making such an assertion in his story.

What Cannon found was the opposite. In total, *RealClearPolitics* ran 374 news stories or opinion pieces on its front page between November 4 and November 17, the day the *New York Times* went after *RealClearPolitics*.

Sixteen of those stories were from *New York Times* reporters, including two columns from Maureen Dowd and one from Paul Krugman. The rest were a balance from outlets on the liberal side, such as the *New Yorker* and the *Nation*, conservative outlets such as the *Daily Caller*, and dozens more, including *CBS News*, *USA Today*, the *Wall Street Journal*, *Politico*, and *The Hill*.

Cannon expected Peters to do the same audit. Instead, Peters wrote a distortion, an apparent projection of a personal belief.

Cannon believes that the criticism of *RealClearPolitics* is a classic case of psychological projection. He repeated what he had written in his story: "We tolerate diverse voices where I work. We encourage it. It's our business model and our belief system. That is what journalism is. So is being thorough in your research when you are going to accuse someone of something."[14]

There are hundreds of stories that one could point to after the 2024 election that could be calculated as "the moment" news organizations broke. The truth is, it was a death by a thousand paper cuts, if you will.

The *New York Times*, like CBS News, ABC, CNN, and NBC, is losing ground with its audiences because it has a vacuum in the diversity of thought. The *Times* alone sat back and watched as Bari Weiss, a western Pennsylvania native, was browbeaten into resigning and editorial page editor James Bennet was fired in response to ungodly demands from within the paper, which had decided to populate itself with left-wing staffers who behaved more like activists than tough-as-nails, unbiased reporters.

At the core of the chasm between most of the country and news organizations providing a haven for activists was trust—trust that news outlets would be unbiased and thorough in their reporting.

The problem with national newsrooms for the past twenty-five years is the same problem that other cultural curators in corporations, government, academia, institutions, and entertainment have: their locations are concentrated in the top zip codes in America, which are in the center of wealth and power—specifically, New York, Washington, DC, and Los Angeles.

When Trump said he wanted to "move parts of the sprawling federal bureaucracy to new locations," CNN and the *Washington Post* reported that it would be wildly disruptive.[15] However, voters agreed with Trump; they want these organizations to be disrupted in the same way they want the news organizations to be disrupted.

As Mike Kelly had said, both the Secret Service and the news organizations were about to face a reckoning.

Yes, these organizations were staffed with "the best of the best," from our finest universities, but there was a profound gap in diversity of thought and experience regarding the people they covered.

There are no consequences for how they cover Normalville, Pennsylvania, because they will never encounter someone from Normalville. However, if these reporters covered Kamala Harris or Joe Biden in a negative way, their social circle would shrink.

These organizations assumed that progressivism was above reproach because they were all progressives. As a result, they made skepticism about the movement hands-off. That decision removed the mask and cost them credibility.

Many national news organizations assumed that most Americans believed what they believed, and so the 2024 election would therefore be decided by their worldview. What they missed is that the country has moved center-right, with independent voters, and many people have lost trust in their structure of news delivery. They also missed that big cities like Los Angeles, New York, and DC don't decide who wins election cycles, but people in places like Butler, Pennsylvania, sure do.

Case in point: When *Politico* ran a story following Trump's Madison Square Garden rally, the news outlet was apparently convinced that because its reporters had read on WhatsApp that Puerto Rican voters in Allentown, Pennsylvania, were bolting from Trump and that could cost him the election, they didn't need to send anyone to Allentown to interview people. Had they done so, they would have found that this was not the case.

That is just one small incident, but it is big in reality.

A 2024 Pew Research Center survey showed that the news media was one of the least-trusted institutions in the United States, a sharp decline from the 1950s when it was among the most trusted institutions.[16]

The survey underscores my earlier point about the *News-Gazette* in Virginia: Americans generally trust local news organizations, but the big guys? Not at all.

Gallup's polling trends show that our trust in media began to crater from a high point in 1973. Then came Watergate, the Pentagon Papers, and the Vietnam War, and a slow collapse began.

As 2024 drew to a close, one thing was certain: newsrooms in America were facing a reckoning. In October, just before Election Day, *Washington Post* owner Jeff Bezos pulled the plug on an endorsement of Kamala Harris, a decision that reportedly prompted two hundred thousand people to cancel their digital subscriptions.

Bezos seemed unmoved. He penned an editorial in the paper, saying, "Most people believe the media is biased" and that "presidential endorsements do nothing to tip the scales of an election. What presidential endorsements actually do is create a perception of bias. A perception of non-independence. Ending them is a principled decision, and it's the right one."[17]

One week before Election Day, a Media Research Center study showed that coverage of the presidential race between former President Donald Trump and Vice President Kamala Harris on *ABC*, *CBS*, and *NBC News* had been "the most lopsided in history."[18]

Analysis from the Media Research Center showed that while Harris had enjoyed 78 percent positive coverage on broadcast evening news since July, Trump had been the subject of 85 percent negative coverage on the same networks.[19]

Voters not only noticed; they moved with their feet over to the world of podcasting, with Joe Rogan at the center of it. Trump sat with Rogan for an interview that lasted more than three hours. Over forty million people downloaded it over three days, and it was likely the moment that solidified change for my profession.

In Pittsburgh, Trump was told during his rally the night before the election that Rogan had endorsed him.

One month later, on an episode of his wildly popular podcast, Rogan summed up the reckoning by arguing that the establishment media that once was friendly to President-elect Donald Trump had since engaged in a years-long psyop, a psychological military strategy that uses information to influence the behavior of others, to convince Americans that Trump is dangerous.

Rogan recalled how friendly people in entertainment and the media once were to Trump. He pointed to Trump's 2012 appearance on *The View* where the panelists fawned over him, and a visit to the *Oprah* show, during which Oprah Winfrey asked Trump if he was thinking about running for president.

What you saw with Trump, Rogan said, regardless of his flaws, was a massive concentrated psychological operation in which many in the media evidently decided to distort people's perceptions of him.

Rogan argued that the 2024 election shows the tide has turned for the national media: "They had control of the media up until now. This election was the first time they didn't really have control of the media anymore."[20]

It is a reckoning.

Afterword

BUTLER, *Pennsylvania*

Early in the morning on October 5, 2024, I saw perched along the rim overlooking the Butler Farm Show Complex hundreds of first responders, most of them volunteer firefighters, standing within feet of their vehicles large and small ready to respond to anything that day.

All of them belonged to different volunteer fire companies, including paramedics who served communities spread throughout Butler County. They were all wearing fluorescent yellow vests emblazoned with "PA EMS STRIKE TEAM" in orange piping. They were ready to serve when duty called.

They could see from their perch the simple but poignant memorial for Corey Comperatore on the stage where he had sat weeks ago when he was struck down by Thomas Crooks; they knew him, and many had served with him in his role as a fire captain. He was part of their community; he was family.

When I went up along the ridge to talk to them, I told them I would be interviewing Trump before the rally. They asked to convey one message to him: "Never forget us."

He didn't.

Three months later, many of those same first responders were the first people President Trump saw at his inauguration parade in Capital One Arena as they carried Comperatore's jacket, the same jacket Trump brought on stage at the Republican National Convention and had displayed in the stands in Butler in October.

There was a moment of silence during the parade to honor Comperatore.

The significance of the moment was not lost on anyone there. You could feel it in the air. The women with whom I was watching the ceremonies had tears running down their faces.

Just a slight turn by Trump, and this would have been not just a very different day; it would have been a very different country. History would have been changed in the same way history would have been changed for another future president over two hundred years earlier.

I watched Trump's expression as the moment happened. It was the same one I have seen pass over his features from time to time since July 13, the one where he inwardly acknowledges that someone died because they supported him. Where he inwardly acknowledges that the person who died could have been him. It reminds him of his obligation to live up to his purpose. And of God.

"It is people like Corey who placed me in office," Trump told me months earlier in Harrisburg. "They come from places like Butler," he said again in Indiana.

It wasn't the only moment place was significant during Inauguration Day. When J. D. Vance was sworn in, he placed his hand on the King James Bible once owned by his maternal great-grandmother who was from the deep hollers of Appalachia. She passed it on to Vance's Mee-maw, who gave it to him on the day he left home for the Marine Corps in September of 2003.

Trump never forgot the importance of place in designing his inauguration, and neither did Vance.

On Inauguration Day, I did what I always do—traverse around Pennsylvania to see how people were viewing it. What I found was that people weren't watching the inauguration; they were celebrating it: in homes, hotel lobbies, friends' houses, diners, and pubs.

Years from the day Trump was sworn in for the second time, people who celebrated the day will tell the story of where they were, how they felt, and how they reclaimed enjoying the art of anticipation that had been missing for the past four years. It was that palpable. For them, it had been a very long time since they experienced that dopamine rush of looking ahead when they dreaded what shoe would drop the next day with Joe Biden.

In the days and weeks after the election in November of 2024, I went back to the Butler Farm Show Complex and walked around the grounds, reflecting on that hot July day that changed everything and that balmy October day when Trump returned to showcase the revival that was happening not just here but all across middle America.

Trump has told me in several conversations since both of those days that the people of Butler will always remain dear in his heart "because they represent all that is good about America."

He expressed the same sentiment about the people from the village of East Palestine, just forty-two miles from Butler, who had to wait a year before Biden showed up to acknowledge their fears and concerns.

"They never showed up to see them. Never. It's a shame. I did, I came, I told them I would not forget them and I won't," Trump said.

It is quiet and peaceful on the grounds of the Farm Show Complex most of the year; the racetrack and the pond, largely hidden from view that day, are pleasant to walk around.

The place feels smaller, different, yet here in Butler, the people I spoke to throughout the county say their way of life will likely remain distant and probably misunderstood by the national media in their narratives now and in the years to come.

Despite being the fastest-growing county in the state—and having a rich, diverse population filled with farmers, steelworkers, professional athletes, doctors, and C-suite executives—Butler's lack of proximity from power, wealth, and influence means that its voting preferences will always be seen as peculiar by the national media.[1]

It is important to note that on November 6, 2024, over 83 percent of eligible people in Butler County voted, with a whopping 65 percent supporting Trump over Kamala Harris.[2]

In the days after the election, the national media reflected on what went wrong, beginning with CNN's media analyst Brian Stelter posting on X (after the election results showed both an electoral and popular vote Trump victory): "The election results put an exclamation point on pervasive concerns about distrust and dissatisfaction with the news media."[3]

Stelter then referred to geographic diversity as being part of the problem, something I have been warning people about for decades. Too many journalists live in the same super zip codes of wealth and power in Washington, DC, and New York, while 60 to 80 percent of gettable readers or viewers live within a handful of miles from the home in middle America where they grew up.[4]

Yes, that is a big part of the problem; however, no efforts have been made to fix it.

By the end of 2024, there were notable shakeups within the national media—most of which was just shuffling the same Washington- and New York–based reporters from one national outlet to another—and little recognition that perhaps hiring more reporters from states where elections are decided, like Michigan,

Wisconsin, Florida, and Pennsylvania, might help them with their geographic diversity problem in their reporting.

When Mark Zuckerberg announced a series of changes that shifted Meta to the center in January 2025, the reactions of some journalists, academics, Hollywood producers, and Democratic operatives were universally strident, accompanied by many dramatic public pronouncements that they were fleeing the company's three platforms: Facebook, Instagram, and WhatsApp.[5]

Zuckerberg said he made the changes because "fact-checkers have been too politically biased," have "destroyed more trust than they created," and use a community notes system similar to Elon Musk's X.[6]

In the days and weeks after the election, as Trump's inauguration drew closer, those initial attempts to touch the issue faded; it was as if it remained too hot to the touch for them to go any further.

They couldn't find the salve.

By January 1, 2025, the press shed all curiosity and self-awareness as to why the American public's trust in our profession was at a historic low and decided to continue with what they've always done: report stories that confirm their bias.[7]

The single-most perfect case of that happened right here in Pennsylvania when the *Philadelphia Inquirer* published a story on January 5 with the headline "The Queer People Who Are Buying Guns to Prepare for Trump's America."[8]

The story quoted a couple of self-identified gay people who were buying firearms, suggesting that they were motivated by the coming of President Trump. It took threads of a multitude of different stories and turned the whole thing into a major story in a major Pennsylvania newspaper where it became quantified Republican homophobia.

The story was not only run in numerous other newspapers and news websites across the country; it was also shared over and over again on social media, confirming how this segment of the population feels about Trump.

The Democrats also seemingly shed all curiosity and self-awareness as to why there was a nationwide repudiation of their party and everything it had come to stand for in the past fifteen years. There was a quick arrogance among Democrats that emerged almost immediately despite losing the White House, the US Senate, and the House by doing worse not just in the rural areas but in cities, suburbs, and college towns as well.

Former Bill Clinton adviser James Carville, who was convinced beyond all doubt that Harris would win, said that the way back to earning Middle American voters should begin with "forcing [Republicans] to oppose a raise in the minimum wage to $15 an hour . . . and make Roe v. Wade an economic messaging issue."[9]

That is not why you lost, Mr. Carville.

Our current reporters in the national media do not understand the people who live in Butler. They don't understand how a doctor, a rural farmer, a Hispanic small business owner, and a steelworker from Butler could all be voting the same.

And they are bewildered by how a working-class person of any race—despite being the men and women who build the roads, make the transformers that light your streets, construct your houses, and weld your bridges so you are safe—could possibly be a conservative populist. And they look down on them for their lack of sheepskins on the wall despite how much better these people make their own lives.

They often look at these men and women as a cohort that needs to be reformed and reeducated—if you are the *Philadelphia Inquirer*, you report that they cause fear among people because of their sexual preferences—and if you think these men and women don't notice how they are viewed or reported, you are wrong.

Here in Butler, and also East Palestine, Johnstown, Luzerne County, Erie, Harrisburg, Indiana, and all of the other three thousand counties that moved rightward since the 2020 election cycle, most people take pride in their work ethic, their family ties, and their faith. Their pick-yourself-up-and-do-what-you-have-to-do attitude drives their days, and if their children and grandchildren do better than them, then they have done their job.[10]

They view the loss of local jobs due to automation and bad trade deals as a cause of the fentanyl crisis, the inability to afford a home or even a decent amount of groceries a direct result of inflation caused by too much government spending, and a mental health crisis among their children coming from overextended pandemic rules.

They watch in horror the growth of gangs from an open border and the spread of homelessness in the bigger cities, a direct result of lawmakers abstaining from enforcing laws on the books.

They blame the press for minimizing these issues or not reporting them at all and the Democrats for having power when they happened.

The people in Butler tell me they don't know what the answer is for the press, and they don't think the Democrats get why it happened and have found a way to get used to it.

"Everything has changed," Jondavid Longo, mayor of Slippery Rock, told me regarding how people view the press and how they believe their lives have been covered in the media.

I don't think we can put the genie back in the bottle. And maybe the moral of what happened in Pennsylvania is, maybe we shouldn't try to.

What I know is the voters in places like Butler are the people who decide the elections, not the people in Washington, in New York. So maybe if the press listened to some of the wisdom coming the middle of the country in places like Butler rather than viewing us as something that needs to be changed that would be a good starting point.

Acknowledgments

First, I'd like to thank my grandparents on both sides of the family, who passed their love for rich storytelling to me. While each came from wildly different experiences, the Zitos escaping poverty at the turn of the twentieth century from Italy, the McJunkins doing so centuries earlier from Ireland, those qualities and gifts they possessed and shared instilled in me an inspiration to become a writer.

A profound thank you to my children Glenn and Shannon; without them, I would not be the person I am—perhaps saner, but definitely much less of a person. Their exuberance in experiencing everything life has to offer, their devotion to each other and to our faith, preserving our family traditions, and pulling pranks on me remind me daily that I got one thing really, really, right.

A big thank you to two high school kids, Joan and Ron Zito, who met at sixteen, married at twenty-one, had four children, and plowed through some pretty tough economic times yet instilled in all of their children the importance of holding tight to traditions, the importance of maintaining the bonds of family, and the dire consequences of missing Sunday dinner.

To my sisters Heather and Annette, their husbands James and Keith, my brother Tony and his wife Kim, and my nieces and

nephews Nick, Kristin, Phil, and Christina, who are polite in trying to understand just what I do and also respect with just the
right amount of fear the consequences of missing Sunday dinner.

Thank you to my friend Keith Urbahn, who also happens to be
my agent, and his partner Matt Latimer, who both believed in me
and stuck with me despite the amount of times I called instead of
texted, or Snapchatted, or whatever young people are doing today.
Their patience, talent, and wisdom are unparalleled.

Thank you to my book editor Alex Pappas for also believing in
me and teaching me how to use new technologies and not laughing too hard when I admitted I was sorely lacking in several of
them—and for his faith in Butler and my storytelling.

To Brad Todd, who coauthored *The Great Revolt: Inside the Populist Coalition Reshaping American Politics* with me, who still takes
my calls, still listens to my wild hunches about voters, and rewards
me with Bradisms.

To Luke Schroeder, Taylor Van Kirk, and Will Martin, J. D.
Vance's press team; Manuel Bonder, Gov. Josh Shapiro's spokesperson; and Steven Cheung, Susie Wiles, and Chris LaCivita
from Trump's team: a very big thank you for your professionalism
in helping me cover this election cycle and tolerating my endless
phone calls.

To President Donald Trump and the people I covered who
are so often overlooked, who without knowing me opened their
homes, neighborhoods, bowling alleys, diners, churches, and hearts
to me—all of you gave me unique access in covering you and your
lives, and for that I am ever blessed and grateful to see all of you
punch up.

Notes

Introduction

1. Ron Chernow, *Washington: A Life* (New York: Penguin Press, 2010), 31–32.

2. "George Washington and the Beginnings of the French and Indian War," Explore PA History.com, accessed February 17, 2025, https://explorepahistory.com/lesson_background.php?id=1-D-12.

3. "The Diaries of George Washington," Library of Congress, accessed February 17, 2025, https://tile.loc.gov/storage-services/service/mss/mgw/mgwd/wd01/wd01.pdf.

1. One Inch Away

1. Adriana Gomez Licon, "How Trump Credits an Immigration Chart for Saving His Life," Associated Press, October 3, 2024, https://apnews.com/article/immigration-trump-chart-butler-border-67866bd05a894a6bea0d670de2adc4f7.

2. Middle of Somewhere, Butler, Pennsylvania

1. US Census Bureau, "New Data Tool and Research Show Where People Move as Young Adults," July 2022, www.census.gov/library/stories/2022/07/theres-no-place-like-home.html.

2. Pennsylvania Historical and Museum Commission, "Pullman-Standard Car Manufacturing Company of Butler, Pennsylvania Records," www.phmc.state.pa.us/bah/dam/mg/mg393.htm#:~:text=During%20World%20War%20Two%2C%20the%20Butler%20plant,war%2C%20use%20of%20railroads%20began%20to%20decline.

3. Eric Freehling, "Pullman Standard Closure Devastated County," *Butler Eagle*, October 8, 2024, www.butlereagle.com/20241008/pullman-standard-closure-devastated-county.

4. Salena Zito, "Trump's Track to Victory Began When Trail Derailed," *Washington Examiner*, January 22, 2024, https://www.washingtonexaminer.com/opinion/2810431/trumps-track-victory-began-when-train-derailed/.

4. Shattered

1. Federal Bureau of Investigation, "Butler Investigation Evidence Photos," August 28, 2024, www.fbi.gov/news/press-releases/butler-investigation-photos.

2. "Obituary: John N. Frizzi," *Pittsburgh Post-Gazette*, December 4, 2010; "Unreported FBI Crime Stats in Pittsburgh and Pennsylvania Create Gaps and Raise Questions About Police Transparency," *Pittsburgh Post-Gazette*, May 5, 2024, www.post-gazette.com/news/crime-courts/2024/05/05/fbi-crime-stats-pennsylania-pittsburgh-nibrs/stories/202405050088.

3. Federal Bureau of Investigation, "Remarks to Media on the Butler, Pennsylvania Assassination Attempt," July 14, 2024, https://www.fbi.gov/news/speeches/remarks-to-media-on-the-butler-pennsylvania-assassination-attempt.

5. A Front-Row Seat

1. "Woman Pistol-Whipped during Daylight Robbery in Downtown Pittsburgh," November 4, 2019, WTAE.com, https://www.wtae.com/article/point-park-students-alerted-about-robbery-in-downtown-pittsburgh/29680984.

2. "Pittsburgh Police Say They Will No Longer Respond to Calls That Are Not 'in Progress Emergencies' Amid Staffing Shortages," *Daily Mail*, March 11, 2024, https://www.dailymail.co.uk/news/article-13184495/Pittsburgh-police-say-no-longer-respond-calls-not-progress-emergencies-amid-staffing-shortages.html.

3. Rick Earle, "11 Investigates: Pittsburgh Police Overnight Staffing to Be Reduced," WPXI, www.wpxi.com/news/local/11-investigates-pittsburgh-police-overnight-staffing-be-reduced/TYZPTIOAKNDVLHXCQSETEKZUCA/.

4. "No Relief: Pittsburgh Office Market Continues to Struggle with High Vacancy Rates and Little Rent Growth, Report Finds," *Pittsburgh Post-Gazette*, September 24, 2024, www.post-gazette.com/business/development/2024/09/24/pittsburgh-office-market-integra-realty-resources-downtown/stories/202409240037.

5.   "Rally Held in Downtown Pittsburgh After Supreme Court Overturns Roe v. Wade," WTAE.com, www.wtae.com/article/pittsburgh-rally-abortion-supreme-court-roe-v-wade/40412470.

6.   "No Relief: Pittsburgh Office Market Continues to Struggle with High Vacancy Rates and Little Rent Growth, Report Finds," *Pittsburgh Post-Gazette*, September 24, 2024, www.post-gazette.com/business/development/2024/09/24/pittsburgh-office-market-integra-realty-resources-downtown/stories/202409240037.

6. "Now the Fun Begins . . ."

1.   Kyle Cheney (@kyledcheney), X, July 21, 2024, https://x.com/kyledcheney/status/1814148348108013619.

2.   Mark Pocan (@MarkPocan), X, July 19, 2024, https://x.com/MarkPocan/status/1814314693445427203.

3.   Shane Goldmacher and Theodore Schleifer, "Michael Moritz, Democratic Megadonor, Urges Biden Exit: 'Clock Has Run Out,'" *New York Times*, July 19, 2024, https://www.nytimes.com/2024/07/19/us/politics/michael-moritz-biden.html.

4.   "Media Slow to Label Shooting Assassination Attempt," *Newsmax*, July 13, 2024, https://www.newsmax.com/politics/media-trump-assassination/2024/07/13/id/1172409/.

5.   Brad Reed, "Early Claims Trump Hit by Glass Fragments after Shooting Were Incorrect," *Raw Story*, July 14, 2024, www.rawstory.com/trump-was-not-hit-by-glass-fragments/.

6.   Joe Biden (@JoeBiden), X, July 21, 2024, https://x.com/JoeBiden/status/1815080881981190320.

7.   Christopher Cadelago, "Kamala Harris Drops Out of Presidential Race," *Politico*, December 3, 2019, www.politico.com/states/california/story/2019/12/03/kamala-harris-drops-out-of-presidential-race-1230369.

8.   Dan Diamond and Cleve R. Wootson Jr., "Kamala Harris Ran Her Office Like a Prosecutor. Not Everyone Liked That," *Washington Post*, September 6, 2024, www.washingtonpost.com/politics/2024/09/06/harris-veep-boss-management/.

9.   Benjamin Kail, "Pennsylvania Democrats Tout Biden's Legacy, Harris Succession as Republicans Pounce on Disarray," *Pittsburgh Post-Gazette*, July 21, 2024, https://www.post-gazette.com/news/election-2024/2024/07/21/pennsylvania-democrats-tout-biden-legacy-harris-endorsements-disarray/stories/202407210145.

10.   Salena Zito, "Lifetime Pennsylvania Democrats Are Becoming Republicans," *Washington Examiner*, July 23, 2024, https://www.washingtonexaminer.com /opinion/3096631/lifetime-pennsylvania-democrats-are-becoming-republicans/.

11.   Jessica Guay, "New Report Shows Pennsylvania Ranks Worst in U.S. with Inflation on Grocery Store Prices," CBS News Pittsburgh, December 13, 2023, www.cbsnews.com/pittsburgh/news/new-report-shows-pennsylvania-ranks -worst-in-u-s-with-inflation-on-grocery-store-prices/.

12.   Maeve Reston and Ashley Parker, "How Trump Crushed Haley's Momentum—and Came Closer to Clinching the Nomination," *Washington Post*, January 23, 2024, https://www.washingtonpost.com/politics/2024/01/23 /trump-haley-new-hampshire-republican-nominee/.

13.   Ben Smith, "Obama on Small-Town Pa.: Clinging to Religion, Guns, Xenophobia," Ben Smith Blog, *Politico*, April 11, 2008, https://www.politico.com /blogs/ben-smith/2008/04/obama-on-small-town-pa-clinging-to-religion-guns -xenophobia-007737.

14.   "Read Hillary Clinton's 'Basket of Deplorables' Remarks About Donald Trump Supporters," *TIME*, September 10, 2016, https://time.com/4486502 /hillary-clinton-basket-of-deplorables-transcript.

15.   David A. Graham, "Gaffe Track: Hillary's Employment Plan for Coal Miners," *Atlantic*, March 14, 2016, https://www.theatlantic.com/politics /archive/2016/03/gaffe-track-hillarys-employment-plan-for-coal-miners/624681/.

16.   Ryan Teague Beckwith, Michelle Jamrisko, and Jennifer Jacobs, "Biden Denounces Trump MAGA Following as an 'Extremist Movement,'" *Bloomberg*, September 28, 2023, https://www.bloomberg.com/news/articles/2023-09-28 /biden-denounces-trump-maga-following-as-an-extremist-movement; Lauren Gambino, "Biden Warns US Democracy Imperiled by Trump and Maga Extremists, *Guardian*, September 2, 2022.

7. The Return

1.   D'Vera Cohn and Rich Morin, "American Mobility: Who Moves? Who Stays Put? Where's Home?," Pew Research Center, www.pewresearch.org /wp-content/uploads/sites/3/2010/10/Movers-and-Stayers.pdf.

2.   Jordan Fabian and Jenny Leonard, "Biden Says Inflation 'Temporary,' Affirms Fed Independence," *Bloomberg*, July 19, 2021, https://www.bloomberg .com/news/articles/2021-07-19/biden-says-inflation-temporary-affirms-fed-in dependence; Andrew Miller, "Since Biden Admin Called Inflation 'Transitory,'

U.S. Has Seen 13 Straight Months of Soaring Costs," Fox Business, July 15, 2022, https://www.foxbusiness.com/politics/biden-admin-called-inflation-transitory -us-13-straight-months-of-soaring-costs.

8. The Son of Appalachia

1. Meg Kinnard, "Why Harris and Democrats Keep Calling Trump and Vance 'Weird,'" AP, July 31, 2024, https://apnews.com/article/kamala-harris-trump-vance-weird-c54d506d1f533ee7aa455f7b500322c5.

2. David Brooks, "Revolt of the Masses," New York Times, June 28, 2016, www.nytimes.com/2016/06/28/opinion/revolt-of-the-masses.html.

3. Salena Zito, "'Hillbilly Elegy' Author JD Vance Courts Trump Country in Run for Senate," New York Post, February 19, 2022. https://nypost.com/2022/02 /19/hillbilly-elegy-author-jd-vance-courts-trump-voters-in-senate-run/.

4. David A. Graham, "The Art of the Dealer," Atlantic, May 2022, www.theatlantic.com/ideas/archive/2022/05/jd-vance-ohio-senate-trump -cultural-heroin/629754/.

5. Suffolk University, "Poll Highlights Ohio's Razor-Thin U.S. Senate Race," September 13, 2022, www.suffolk.edu/news-features/news/2022/09/13 /16/56/ohio-poll.

6. Nick Kariuki and Emily Neil, "Republican VP Nominee JD Vance Visits South Philly in First Pa. Campaign Stop," WHYY.org, August 6, 2024, https://whyy.org/articles/philadelphia-jd-vance-election-harris/.

7. Ramesh Ponnuru, "J.D. Vance's Demeaning Remarks Don't Help This Valid Cause," Washington Post, August 12, 2024, www.washingtonpost .com/opinions/2024/08/12/jd-vance-childless-cat-ladies-natalism -arguments/.

8. Amelia Robinson, "JD Vance Thinks My Vote Should Count Less. He Should Listen to Jennifer Aniston," Columbus Dispatch, July 26, 2024, www.dis patch.com/story/opinion/columns/2024/07/26/jd-vance-cat-lady-comments -jennifer-aniston-ivf/74543387007/.

9. Andrea Vacchiano, "JD Vance Roasts Harris on Wisconsin Tarmac for Avoiding Press, Calls Air Force 2 His 'Future Plane,'" Fox News, August 7, 2024, https://www.foxnews.com/politics/jd-vance-roasts-harris-wisconsin-tarmac -avoiding-press-calls-air-force-2-his-future-plane.

10. Nia Prater, "Vance Awkwardly Doesn't Confront Harris on Plane Tarmac," New York Magazine Intelligencer, August 7, 2024, https://nymag.com

/intelligencer/article/vance-awkwardly-doesnt-confront-harris-on-plane-tarmac
.html.

11. Josephine Walker, "JD Vance Awkwardly Retreats After Bizarre Attempt to Storm Harris' Empty Plane," *The Daily Beast*, August 7, 2024, www
.thedailybeast.com/jd-vance-awkwardly-retreats-from-confronting-kamala
-harris-on-air-force-2-after-realizing-she-wasnt-around/.

12. "JD Vance Reveals Shocking Chemical Pollution of East Palestine Creek After Train Crash," Forbes Breaking News, February 16, 2023, https://
www.youtube.com/watch?v=Kx6WhlO6J_o.

13. Salena Zito, "The Riddle of JD Vance," *Washington Examiner*, August 4, 2023, https://www.washingtonexaminer.com/news/senate/944918/the-riddle
-of-jd-vance/.

14. Salena Zito, "A Year Later, East Palestine, Ohio, Still Suffers," *Wall Street Journal*, February 15, 2024, https://www.wsj.com/articles/jd-vance-shows
-his-nonpartisan-side-in-east-palestine-train-derailment-safety-ohio-9cdc9aaf.

15. "Vice President Harris Says She Was the Last Person in the Room with President Biden When He Made the Afghanistan Troop Withdrawal Decision," CNN, August 2021, https://www.facebook.com/watch/?v=279956343606334.

16. Salena Zito, "What Really Happened to JD Vance in Erie," *Washington Examiner*, August 29, 2024, https://www.washingtonexaminer.com/opinion
/columnists/3138057/what-really-happened-vance-erie/.

17. Tim Haines, "JD Vance: 'I Don't Need A Teleprompter, I've Actually Got Thoughts In My Head, Unlike Kamala Harris,'" *RealClearPolitics*, August 28, 2024, https://www.realclearpolitics.com/video/2024/08/28/jd_vance_i_dont
_need_a_teleprompter_ive_actually_got_thoughts_in_my_head_unlike_kamala
_harris.html.

18. "#2221 JD Vance," Joe Rogan Experience, October 31, 2024, https://
www.youtube.com/watch?v=fRyyTAs1XY8.

9. There Is No There There . . .

1. Salena Zito, "Harris's Tightly Controlled Pennsylvania Event Avoided Pittsburgh," *Washington Examiner*, August 19, 2024, https://www.washington
examiner.com/opinion/3125951/harris-tightly-controlled-pennsylvania-event
-avoided-pittsburgh/.

2. Helen Fallon, "Dispel Those Rumors: Jefferson Hills Couple Recount Meeting Harris and Walz at Moon Campaign Bus Tour," *Pittsburgh Union*

Progress, August 27, 2024, www.unionprogress.com/2024/08/27/dispel-those-ru-mors-jefferson-hills-couple-recount-meeting-harris-and-walz-at-moon-cam-paign-bus-tour/.

3. "Harris and Walz Make Small-Town Stops and Campaign Phone Calls on Pennsylvania Bus Tour Before DNC," *U.S. News & World Report*, August 18, 2024, www.usnews.com/news/politics/articles/2024-08-18/harris-and-walz -will-campaign-by-bus-in-pennsylvania-before-the-democratic-convention-in -chicago.

4. "Cross-Tabs: August 2024 Times/Siena Poll of Registered Voters in Pennsylvania," *New York Times*, August 10, 2024, https://www.nytimes.com /interactive/2024/08/10/us/elections/times-siena-poll-pennsylvania-registered -voters.html.

5. "Kennedy's Decision Is Unlikely to Change the Race Significantly," *New York Times*, August 22, 2024, https://www.nytimes.com/2024/08/22/us /elections/kennedy-polls-trump-endorsement-effect.html.

6. Lisa Lerer and Michael Gold, "Trump Spreads His Politics of Griev-ance to Non-White Voters," *New York Times*, October 10, 2024, https://www .nytimes.com/2024/10/10/us/politics/trump-voters-black-latino.html.

7. Mike Wendling, "RFK Jr Just Endorsed Trump. Will It Matter in November?" *BBC*, August 23, 2024, https://www.bbc.com/news/articles/c3d9rj 33x1no.

8. Bret Stephens, "A Vague, Vacuous TV Interview Didn't Help Kamala Harris," *New York Times*, August 29, 2024, www.nytimes.com/live/2024/08/27 /opinion/thepoint?timespastHighlight=bret,stephens#harris-walz-interview.

9. SAG-AFTRA, "Pittsburgh Labor Day Parade & Picnic," www.sagaftra .org/pittsburgh-labor-day-parade-picnic.

10. Stephen Collinson, "Biden Hears Labor Day Cheers: 'Run, Joe, Run,'" CNN, September 7, 2015, https://www.cnn.com/2015/09/07/politics/joe-biden -2016-labor-day/index.html.

11. Mary Alice Salinas, "Biden Decides Against 2016 Presidential Run," VOA News, October 21, 2015, https://www.voanews.com/a/biden-decides-not -to-run-for-president/3016958.htm.

12. Bureau of Labor Statistics, "Union Members in Pennsylvania—2023," www.bls.gov/regions/mid-atlantic/news-release/unionmembership_pennsylva nia.htm.

13. "Salena Zito: How the Democratic Establishment Gave Way to a New Generation of Progressives," *Pittsburgh Post-Gazette*, May 21, 2023, https://

www.post-gazette.com/opinion/insight/2023/05/21/sara-innamorato-alleghe
ny-county-executive-bethany-hallam-mik-pappas/stories/202305210035.

14. Chris Potter, "Harris, Biden Share the Stage, and an Agenda, at Pittsburgh Labor Day Appearance with Union Members," WESA.fm, September
2, 2024, https://www.wesa.fm/politics-government/2024-09-02/harris-biden
-agenda-labor-day-pittsburgh-union.

15. Lindsay Kornick, "Local Pennsylvania Reporters Were Told by Harris
Campaign to 'Not Disrupt' Tim Walz Event," September 4, 2024, Fox News,
https://www.foxnews.com/media/local-pennsylvania-reporters-were-told-har
ris-campaign-not-disrupt-tim-walz-event.

16. Kornick, "Local Pennsylvania Reporters."

17. Taylor Millard, "Poll: 58% of PA Voters Oppose Biden's LNG Export
Ban," *Delaware Valley Journal*, March 4, 2024, https://delawarevalleyjournal.com
/poll-58-of-pa-voters-oppose-bidens-lng-export-ban/.

18. Aaron Pellish (@aaronpellish), X, September 5, 2024, https://x.com
/aaronpellish/status/1831701218005070050?s=46&t=8x84ZTFJMHgE6-j
Qr7nJwA.

19. Melissa Koenig, "Penzeys Spices CEO Sparks Fury by Renaming MLK
Day 'Republicans are RACIST Weekend,'" Daily Mail.com, January 18, 2022,
https://www.dailymail.co.uk/news/article-10414483/Penzeys-Spices-CEO
-slammed-renames-MLK-Day-Republicans-racist-weekend.html.

20. "Remarks by Vice President Harris in Press Gaggle, Pittsburgh, PA,"
The White House, September 7, 2024, https://bidenwhitehouse.archives.gov
/briefing-room/speeches-remarks/2024/09/07/remarks-by-vice-president-harris
-in-press-gaggle-pittsburgh-pa-2/.

21. @jameshohmann, X, September 7, 2024, https://x.com/jameshohmann
/status/1832489842862944333?s=43&t=8x84ZTFJMHgE6-jQr7nJwA.

22. Darlene Superville, "Harris Turns to Her Favorite Foods in Effort to
Show a More Private Side and Connect with Voters," AP, September 8, 2024,
https://apnews.com/article/harris-doritos-collard-greens-root-beer-food-82956
ec65fcf24e6c57712716845d2af?utm_campaign=TrueAnthem&utm_medium=
AP&utm_source=Twitter.

23. "Harris Makes Stop at Pittsburgh Business Amid Debate Preparation,"
MSNBC, September 7, 2024, https://www.msnbc.com/weekends-with-alex-witt

/watch/harris-makes-stop-at-pittsburgh-business-amid-debate-preparation -218827333569.

24. Emma Bowman, "Obama, in Blunt Terms, Tells Black Men to Get Over Their Reluctance to Support Harris," NPR, October 10, 2024, https:// www.npr.org/2024/10/10/g-s1-27633/barack-obama-kamala-harris-black-men -pennsylvania.

10. "As I Was Saying. . ."

1. Salena Zito, "Elon Musk Says 'Destiny of America' Is on the Line," *Washington Examiner*, October 6, 2024, https://www.washingtonexaminer .com/opinion/3178774/exclusive-elon-musk-says-destiny-of-america-is-on-the -line/.

2. Salena Zito, "Elon Musk Says 'Destiny of America' Is on the Line."

3. Jeffrey Goldberg, "Trump: 'I Need the Kind of Generals That Hitler Had,'" *Atlantic*, October 22, 2024, www.theatlantic.com/politics/archive/2024/10 /trump-military-generals-hitler/680327/.

11. "There Will Never Be Another One Like Him. . ."

1. Jeffrey Goldberg, "Trump: 'I Need the Kind of Generals That Hitler Had,'" *Atlantic*, October 22, 2024, https://www.theatlantic.com/politics/archive /2024/10/trump-military-generals-hitler/680327/.

2. Michael S. Schmidt, "As Election Nears, Kelly Warns Trump Would Rule Like a Dictator," *New York Times*, October 22, 2024, www.nytimes.com /2024/10/22/us/politics/john-kelly-trump-fitness-character.html.

3. Salena Zito, "Harris Struggles to Shine Thanks to Biden Garbage," *Washington Examiner*, October 30, 2024, www.washingtonexaminer.com/opinion /3210319/harris-struggles-to-shine-thanks-to-biden-garbage.

4. Jeffery C. Mays, "Is Trump a Fascist? This Time, Mayor Adams Dodges the Question," *New York Times*, October 29, 2024, www.nytimes.com/2024/10/29 /nyregion/adams-trump-fascist-msg.html.

5. Ruby Cramer, "Trump Is 'Fascist to the Core,' Milley Says in Wood-ward Book," *Washington Post*, October 12, 2024, www.washingtonpost.com/nation /2024/10/12/mark-milley-donald-trump-fascist/.

6. Joshua Zeitz, "Trump and Fascism: A Pair of Historians Tackle the Big Question," *Politico*, October 29, 2024, www.politico.com/news/magazine/2024 /10/29/trump-fascism-historians-00186027.

7. April Rubin, "Trump's Top General Calls Former President 'Fascist' and 'Dangerous' Threat," *Axios*, October 11, 2024, www.axios.com/2024/10/11 /mark-milley-trump-fascist-bob-woodward-book.

8. Erin Doherty, "Harris Says She Believes Trump Is a Fascist at CNN Town Hall," *Axios*, October 24, 2024, www.axios.com/2024/10/24/harris-trump -fascist-cnn-town-hall.

9. Morning Joe (@morningjoe), Instagram, "It's Time That Fascism Is Called Fascism and Americans Know Exactly What They're Voting For," www .instagram.com/morningjoe/reel/Cz60kE6AyMC/.

10. Julia Cherner, "Mark Cuban Says Trump 'Absolutely' Has 'Fascist Tendencies,'" ABC News, October 27, 2024, https://abcnews.go.com/Politics/mark -cuban-trump-absolutely-fascist-tendencies/story?id=115181894.

11. Shane Goldmacher, Maggie Haberman, and Michael Gold, "Trump at the Garden: A Closing Carnival of Grievances, Misogyny and Racism," *New York Times*, October 27, 2024, www.nytimes.com/2024/10/27/us/trump-msg-rally.html.

12. Joey Garrison, "'Fixated on His Grievances': Harris Blasts Trump's Madison Square Garden Rally," *USA Today*, October 28, 2024, https://www.usatoday .com/story/news/politics/elections/2024/10/28/harris-blasts-trumps-madison -square-garden-rally/75898034007/.

13. Meredith Lee Hill, Mia McCarthy, and Holly Otterbein, "Trump's Puerto Rico Fallout Is 'Spreading Like Wildfire' in Pennsylvania," *Politico*, October 28, 2024, www.politico.com/news/2024/10/28/trump-rally-puerto-rico -pennsylvania-fallout-00185935.

14. "Trump Reacts on Stage to Biden's 'Garbage' Comments," CNN.com, October 29, 2024, https://www.cnn.com/2024/10/29/politics/video/biden-trump -supporters-garbage-white-house-digvid.

15. Zito, "Harris Struggles to Shine."

16. "Biden Defends Puerto Ricans," *Politico*, October 29, 2024, https:// www.politico.com/live-updates/2024/10/29/2024-elections-live-coverage-up dates-analysis/biden-defends-puerto-ricans-00186165.

17. "Biden Appears to Insult Trump Supporters as 'Garbage,'" *New York Times*, October 29, 2024, https://www.nytimes.com/2024/10/29/us/politics/biden -garbage-trump-supporters.html.

18. Zito, "Harris Struggles to Shine."

19. Zito, "Harris Struggles to Shine."

20. Salena Zito (@ZitoSalena), X, November 4, 2024, https://x.com/Zito Salena/status/1853572676972945485.

21. Salena Zito, "There Will Never Be Another One Like Him," *Washington Examiner*, November 5, 2024, www.washingtonexaminer.com/opinion /columnists/3217761/there-will-never-be-another-one-like-him.

22. Zito, "There Will Never Be Another One Like Him."

23. Zito, "There Will Never Be Another One Like Him."

24. Zito, "There Will Never Be Another One Like Him."

25. Zito, "There Will Never Be Another One Like Him."

12. The Reckoning

1. Sasha Pezenik, Josh Margolin, and Riley Hoffman, "Trump's Would-Be Assassin's Father Called 911 Looking for Son Hours After Shooting: 'We're Kind of Worried,'" ABC News, December 5, 2024, https://abcnews.go.com/US /trumps-assassins-father-called-911-son-hours-after/story?id=116505119.

2. United States House of Representatives, *Task Force on the Attempted Assassination of Donald J. Trump: Final Report of Findings and Recommendations*, December 5, 2024.

3. Jim VandeHei and Mike Allen, "Behind the Curtain: The Big Media Era Is Over," *Axios*, October 28, 2024, www.axios.com/2024/10/28/election-news -media-trump-harris.

4. Northwestern University, "Local News Initiative," https://localnewsini tiative.northwestern.edu/.

5. Salena Zito, "Where Our Trust in News Lives," *Washington Examiner*, January 24, 2020, www.washingtonexaminer.com/news/1562121/where-our -trust-in-news-lives/.

6. Carl M. Cannon, "The Mourning Paper: Delivering News of RFK's Death," *RealClearPolitics*, June 8, 2018, www.realclearpolitics.com/articles/2018 /06/08/the_mourning_paper_delivering_news_of_rfks_death_137239.html.

7. Carl M. Cannon, "The New York Times vs. RealClearPolitics," *RealClearPolitics*, April 4, 2024, www.realclearpolitics.com/articles/2024/04/04/the _new_york_times_vs_realclearpolitics_150733.html.

8. Ari L. Goldman, "Catholic Bishops Defend Their Actions to Combat Child Abuse by Priests," *New York Times*, February 10, 1988, www.nytimes

.com/1988/02/10/us/catholic-bishops-defend-their-actions-to-combat-child
-abuse-by-priests.html.

9.　Jacob Heilbrunn, "What Would Reagan Do?," *New York Times*, March
2, 2008, www.nytimes.com/2008/03/02/books/review/Heilbrunn2-t.html.

10.　Peter J. Henning, "Behind the Rise and Fall of a Class Action King,"
New York Times, March 1, 2010, https://archive.nytimes.com/dealbook.nytimes
.com/2010/03/01/behind-the-rise-and-fall-of-a-class-action-king/.

11.　Carl M. Cannon, "Disclosed," *New York Times*, September 2, 2007,
www.nytimes.com/2007/09/02/books/review/Cannon-t.html.

12.　Cannon, "The New York Times vs. RealClearPolitics."

13.　Jeremy Peters, "A Popular Political Site Made a Sharp Right Turn.
What Steered It?" *New York Times*, November 17, 2020, https://www.nytimes
.com/2020/11/17/us/politics/real-clear-politics.html.

14.　Cannon, "The New York Times vs. RealClearPolitics."

15.　CNN, Transcript of 2–3 am ET, April 29, 2024, https://transcripts.cnn
.com/show/cnr/date/2024-04-29/segment/19.

16.　Pew Research Center, "Trust in America: Do Americans Trust the News
Media?" January 5, 2022, https://www.pewresearch.org/journalism/2022/01/05
/trust-in-america-do-americans-trust-the-news-media/.

17.　Jon Talton, "Jeff Bezos Killing The Washington Post's Endorsement
Tarnishes His Legacy," *Seattle Times*, November 1, 2024, https://www.seattle
times.com/business/jeff-bezos-killing-the-washington-posts-endorsement
-tarnishes-his-legacy/.

18.　Howard Kurtz, "Why Trump, Battling Media Hostility, Is Declar-
ing War on Fact-Checkers," Fox News, October 16, 2024, www.foxnews.com
/politics/why-trump-battling-media-hostility-declaring-war-fact-checkers.

19.　Rich Noyes, "TV Hits Trump with 85% Negative News vs. 78% Positive Press for Harris," *NewsBusters*, October 28, 2024, https://newsbusters
.org/blogs/nb/rich-noyes/2024/10/28/tv-hits-trump-85-negative-news-vs-78
-positive-press-harris.

20.　Mike Bedigan, "Joe Rogan Claims a 'Media Psy-Op' Is Responsible for
People Having a Negative View of Trump," *Independent*, November 30, 2024,
https://www.independent.co.uk/news/world/americas/us-politics/joe-rogan
-trump-psy-op-b2656584.html.

Afterword

1. Butler County Chamber of Commerce, "About the County," www
.butlercountychamber.com/new-page-3#:~:text=Butler%20County%2C%20
nestled%20in%20the,a%20testament%20to%20its%20appeal.

2. Butler County, Pennsylvania, "Summary Results Report, 2024 Presidential General, November 5, 2024," www.butlercountypa.gov/DocumentCenter
/View/9560/ELECTION-SUMMARY-PDF.

3. Brian Stelter (@BrianStelter), X, November 16, 2024, https://x.com
/brianstelter/status/1857826940180123893.

4. Nathaniel Hendren, Sonya R. Porter, and Ben Sprung-Keyser, "New
Data Tool and Research Show Where People Move as Young Adults," US Census Bureau, July 25, 2022, www.census.gov/library/stories/2022/07/theres-no
-place-like-home.html#:~:text=Nearly%20six%20in%2010%20young,far%20
from%20their%20childhood%20home.

5. Kristine Parks, "Liberal Media Commentators Rage After Meta Ends
Fact-Checking Program: 'Incredibly Dangerous,'" Fox News, January 8, 2025,
www.foxnews.com/media/liberal-media-commentators-rage-after-meta-ends
-fact-checking-program-incredibly-dangerous.

6. "Meta Says Fact-Checkers Were the Problem," *New York Times*,
January 7, 2025, https://www.nytimes.com/2025/01/07/business/mark-zuckerberg
-meta-fact-check.html.

7. Megan Brenan, "Americans' Trust in Media Remains at a Trend Low,"
Gallup News, October 14, 2024, https://news.gallup.com/poll/651977/americans
-trust-media-remains-trend-low.aspx.

8. Zoe Greenberg, "The Queer People Who Are Buying Guns to Prepare
for Trump's America," *Philadelphia Inquirer*, January 5, 2025, www.inquirer.com
/identity/guns-trump-lgbt-philadelphia-20250105.html.

9. James Carville, "I Was Wrong about the 2024 Election. Here's Why,"
New York Times, January 2, 2025, https://www.nytimes.com/2025/01/02/opinion
/democrats-donald-trump-economy.html.

10. Reid J. Epstein, Lisa Lerer, and Nicholas Nehamas, "Devastated Democrats Play the Blame Game, and Stare at a Dark Future," *New York Times*, November 7, 2024, www.nytimes.com/2024/11/07/us/politics/democrats-kamala-harris
.html.

About the Author

Salena Zito is a veteran political reporter with more than twenty years of award-winning experience in print and broadcast journalism. With her trusty Jeep that shows four hundred thousand miles on the odometer and a refusal to travel on interstates, Zito is a reporter who harkens to an older generation of journalism, one that listens to the stories of everyday Americans in places far outside the artificial bubbles of Manhattan and the Beltway. This willingness to travel and listen made Zito one of the only journalists to understand the outcome of the 2016 election long before her peers. One of the last scribes of middle America, she famously identified the root cause of the media's failed coverage and underestimation of Donald Trump by concluding, "The press takes him literally, but not seriously; his supporters take him seriously, but not literally." Zito is a national political reporter for the *Washington Examiner*, a post she has held since 2016, and is a regular contributor to the *Wall Street Journal*. She was previously a columnist at the *New York Post* and the *Atlantic*. Throughout her career, she has been a reporter and columnist for the *Pittsburgh Post-Gazette* and the *Pittsburgh Tribune Review*, where her columns are must-reads for those seeking to understand the Pennsylvania political landscape. Her columns have been syndicated in more than two hundred local, regional, and national newspapers nationwide. Zito was a CNN contributor for five years and remains a frequent broadcast guest for her insights on the American electorate.